Discombobulated:
an Inspiring Journey of Hope Through Mental Illness

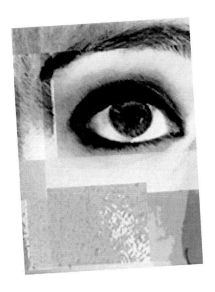 

Written by:
Kelly Ann Compton

Contributor: Cheryl Arnold, Ph.D.

Order this book online at www.trafford.com/05-3167
or email orders@trafford.com

Most Trafford titles are also available at major online book retailers.

Note for Librarians: A cataloguing record for this book is available from Library
and Archives Canada at www.collectionscanada.ca/amicus/index-e.html

Printed in Victoria, BC, Canada.

ISBN: 978-1-4120-8201-3

*We at Trafford believe that it is the responsibility of us all, as both individuals
and corporations, to make choices that are environmentally and socially sound.
You, in turn, are supporting this responsible conduct each time you purchase a
Trafford book, or make use of our publishing services. To find out how you are
helping, please visit www.trafford.com/responsiblepublishing.html*

*Our mission is to efficiently provide the world's finest, most comprehensive
book publishing service, enabling every author to experience success.
To find out how to publish your book, your way, and have it available
worldwide, visit us online at www.trafford.com/10510*

 www.trafford.com

North America & international
toll-free: 1 888 232 4444 (USA & Canada)
phone: 250 383 6864 ✦ fax: 250 383 6804 ✦ email: info@trafford.com

The United Kingdom & Europe
phone: +44 (0)1865 722 113 ✦ local rate: 0845 230 9601
facsimile: +44 (0)1865 722 868 ✦ email: info.uk@trafford.com

10 9 8 7 6 5 4 3

About the Authors

Kelly Ann Compton shares her own story in *Discombobulated: an inspiring journey of hope through mental illness*. With her recovery, Kelly Ann has had a passion to share the hope of her story and perhaps bring hope to others having a mental illness. She wrote *Discombobulated* because it crashed into her brain screaming to be written. Kelly Ann has been a special education teacher for twenty years. She holds an M.S.Ed. in special education and an MA in counseling. Free time finds Kelly Ann sewing, reading and movie watching.

Dr. Cheryl Arnold is a psychologist and educator in Denver, Colorado. Her areas of expertise include eating disorders and Dissociative Identity Disorder (aka Multiple Personality Disorder.) In addition to national television appearances on Montel, Dr. Arnold has presented at national and international conferences in the areas of psychology and education. She holds a doctoral degree in Counseling Psychology. In her spare time, Dr. Arnold enjoys traveling the world and spending time with family.

FOR CHERYL, WITH A
GRATEFUL HEART

Heartfelt thanks to: Mary, Patti,
Donna, Kelly B., Debbie, Pat, Bev, and Jim.
Without you my book would not have happened.

Discombobulated:

an Inspiring Journey of Hope Through Mental Illness

Be joyful in hope,
patient in affliction,
faithful in prayer.

Romans 12:12

PREFACE

Emotion is a gift from God. We were created to feel. This gift can be validated by looking at God's own Son. Jesus wept. Jesus loved. Jesus expressed anger. Given these facts, it should be evident that not only were we created to feel, we are allowed to feel and know what those feelings are. Hopefully, we also know what to do with our feelings.

For some people, things happen either externally or internally to mess up their ability to recognize and deal with their emotions. Emotions become a tangled, sometimes unidentifiable mass of pain-filled crossed wires traveling through tunnels of pain darker than a starless, moonless night. Emotions become an enemy of torture with the wires shorting out in spasms until the feeling of craziness sets in, and with it a mental illness. Such is the true story that follows.

This true story tells of my own journey through the world of mental illness. While I give my story to you freely, it is also a private story. Therefore, all names have been changed to protect the private lives of each and every person referred to. I refer to myself as Lili Marie Warner as that is the name I used for myself in frequent journal entries.

Throughout my journey I questioned God. What would be the outcome of my mental illness? What was I to do with this journey of mine? Then one day in an Old Testament class, we read I Samuel and I met Hannah.

Hannah was a barren married woman. She loved her husband and was loved in return. The only thing Hannah wanted was to bear a child, a son. She seemed depressed as she prayed to God for a son. Being loved by her husband was not enough. To add fuel to her pain, she was harassed, first by other women who knew her torment and then by a priest who mistook her prayerfulness for drunkenness. Even her husband harassed her asking "Am I not more to you than ten sons?"

The themes of Hannah's story struck a chord within me: wanting, praying, asking, promising. None of these things surprised me. We all want, pray, ask and promise. We all have tried to make deals with God. God, just give me this, and I will ….

I wasn't surprised by the ways in which Hannah was misunderstood. I wasn't surprised that she prayed for a son and in that prayer promised to give that son back to God. It didn't even surprise me that God granted her deepest desire and gave her a son to bear. No, what surprised me was what

Hannah did next. Hannah kept her promise. She gave the baby, Samuel, back to God by giving him to the priest to raise. Awesome. The one thing Hannah wanted most in the world she gave up to and for God. This awed my mind and answered the question that had perplexed me. What to do with my mental illness, what to do with my recovery. Hannah gave the one thing she wanted back to God. I wanted sanity. It became my purpose to give my sanity back to God. Whatever gift I received from God, I was going to give back to him.

God gifted me with the recovery of mental health. With this gift came the urge, the passion, the need to tell my story. I had to write it down. Every time I felt at loose ends with life, a compelling presence filled me with the words, "Tell your story. It needs to be told." I believe that by telling my story I am returning my gift to God. I hope that by sharing my story some good might come. Perhaps a better understanding of someone you love. Perhaps a sigh of relief that you are not alone.

Kelly Ann Compton

Prologue

I have been deemed sane and stable by my therapist of nine years. Hannah Lee, the therapist, decided to become Ms. Famous World Traveler and closed down her psychology practice. I knew in my heart that I no longer needed intense weekly therapy, but it pissed me off that Ms. Hannah Lee was dumping me. I mean, didn't our nine years together mean anything to her? One day she was my confidant and emotional mentor; the next she was Hannah Lee: Ms. Famous World Traveler. It sucked.

I admit that I don't need the intense therapy anymore, but do I have to give up the most stable environment and relationship I have ever had? So I write this book to see if she is right. I hold a definite ambivalence toward the thought of being sane and stable while Hannah Lee runs off to be Ms. Famous World Traveler.

Oh, Hannah Lee, why must YOU flee?

Beginnings

Why are you downcast, O my soul?
Why so disturbed within me?
Put your hope in God,
for I will yet praise him,
my Savior and my God.

Psalm 42:5

One

It is not easy going crazy. Contrary to what people think, one does not go crazy all at once. I have been working on it for years, and I am still not completely looney. In fact, most people would not believe me if I told them that I am looney. For a minimum of ten years, I have been working on entering the world of non reality. My mind is in a constant state of twists and hallways. Thoughts keep trying to hide from each other, and yet they continue to find each other. It is amazing, really. I know that I should get some help, but frankly, I do not think anyone would believe me. Then my mind wears out and wishes that I could stop thinking just for a short time. My concentration is off. I guess I should say that it is missing. I do not seem able to concentrate for long periods of time any more. Part of it is an addiction to television. My attention drifts. If I turn off the television, I go crazy from the noise of my own thoughts. My mind would like to rest. It is time for a nap.[1]

My 34th birthday holds the sweetest of memories—except for the part that proved to be the beginning of my worst years. XY and I were best friends. (XY's name is Weston. The fact is, thinking of him by name is simply too painful for me. Therefore, I do not call him by any name.) We shared a birthday month. On his birthday I taught him the right-hand part to Bach's "Invention in F." We sat side by side on the piano bench for what seemed like hours playing the same song—or part of a song—over and over. It was wonderful. One night, several days before my birthday, XY surprised me with an early birthday adventure. He drove us up to Boulder Falls, and we climbed the uneven stone steps up to the falls in the dark. When we reached the falls we sat on a

---

ALL INSET PASSAGES ARE JOURNAL ENTRIES. THE LILI STORIES, ALSO INSET, ARE JOURNAL ENTRIES WHERE I WROTE OUT MY EXPERIENCES AS IF TELLING MYSELF A STORY.

rock and listened. The October air was fresh and crisp. The rock we sat on chilled our buns. Here we were alone on a mountain breathing in the fresh scents of pine and water, listening to the falls rush and crash into the rocky river below. It felt romantic. In response to the romantic mood, I reached out to take XY's hand. He pulled away. Laughing, my hand reached out again. Once more, XY pulled away. We ended up in a laughing hand fight. This should have been a clue. I thought he was being shy. I was wrong. Merely one month later the joy of our friendship would disappear, and my life of constant crisis would erupt. A year later, I was being released from a psych ward.

Having been declared safe, it was my first night home from the hospital. No longer was I considered a danger to myself or others. I guess I was safe. Safer than before anyway. On my drive home everything felt fresh and new. Every building seemed to have extra-sharp clear lines and corners. The sky was a cloudless robin's egg blue. No longer would I be stuck on a single floor of a hospital psych unit. No. Now I could soar along the highway free, free, free! The hospital had been a very interesting place. I had hated it, yet felt very safe—like that was where I belonged. And now I was home.

Getting ready to sleep in my own bed felt even more freeing. Crawling between my cool, clean sheets with smooth freshly shaven legs felt luxurious. Oh, it felt good. I was home at last. On my way to or through dreamland, the unexpected occurred. Someone or something latched on to me and held me down. I could not move. My hair was being pulled straight out to the point that my scalp hurt. The room was pitch black giving the feeling that it was the middle of the night. I knew I was wide awake. I knew I was alone.

"Come with me," teased a dark voice. "Come with me."

"Who's there? What do you want?"

"Leave your body and come fly with me," the voice lured, challenged.

What a freeing thought. Why not fly away? I could fly away and be free from my brain, my life. "Yes, I will come. I'll fly away with you."

Wanting desperately to fly with the owner of that seductive voice, I tried to let loose and go. But no matter how hard I tried, I couldn't move. An invisible grip locked me to the bed. Panting, struggling, screaming for release, I fought the hold that held me down.

A strong gentle voice warned, "Don't go. Don't fly away."

"Why not?" I asked, "I want to go. I want to be free."

"It would be wrong to go. Don't go," the gentle voice urged.

Then evil moved in with power yanking my hair, my arms, my legs. The evil attacked me trying to get me to fly. I tried thrashing about, but I couldn't move. My body felt as if electricity was shooting through my every pore. Pins and needles of electricity held me down.

"Help!" My brain pleaded, "Help!"

The struggle lasted for several minutes. Fly. Don't fly. My hair hurt. The electrical shocks pulsed and stung their way through me. Attempting to pull this way and that, I still couldn't move. My mouth began screaming, but no sound came out. The struggle continued painfully for several minutes then POOF! I was alone, no longer held down on my bed. The voices disappeared. Everything seemed calm. The room was still dark, but now the lights of night flickered here and there dancing on the walls. I had no idea of what had just happened, but knew it was not a dream coming from within the depths of sleep. Doctors and counselors would discount this event. For me, the event remains as real as an electromagnet's pulling power.

In many journal entries, I refer to myself as Lili Marie Warner. Using a different name helped me be a little more objective. In the telling of my story, I will continue to call myself Lili. The names of other people have also been changed.

I wasn't always crazy. That is why it is important to back up to the very beginning. I want you to see that mental illness crept upon me slowly, secretly. It developed, for me, over a period of years in snippets and pieces that eventually snowballed themselves into constant crises and craziness. I want you to know that my family was a family filled with love. We weren't perfect by any means, but the love was always strong and binding. In the end, I want you to remember the hope. There was always hope. At times, others would need to hold my hope for me until I was able to grasp hold, but the hope always existed. As we travel through my years of craziness, remember the hope.

The story of my birth has always delighted me. My mother's water broke on Thursday, and I was born the following Tuesday. I have always imagined Dad running after Mother mopping up the floor as the water poured out from her. The birthing process wasn't easy for mother and me. Mother was given Demerol during labor, which threw her into crazy mode. She has told me that she started yelling things that should not leave a lady's lips. The doctor had Dad come into the labor room to try to keep her calm. It must have been bad, for this was the 1950s and fathers were not encouraged to be a part of the birthing process. I ended up being a forceps birth; I have the scar to prove it. When I finally popped out, the good doctor had to leap up and catch me. Mother told me that when she and Dad first got into the car with me, all nervous and wondering what to do with this new little person, they turned on the radio and what should come through the speakers but Jerry Lewis singing "'Rock-a-Bye My Baby' to a Dixie melody." How fun.

My parents say that when I was born they were "Lilified." I guess I took over their lives. I talked and walked early and even managed to potty-train myself by age one. At nine months, I had a fifteen word vocabulary. At ten and a half months, I slipped off my sleeping mother's lap and walked across the street. "I play Debbie," I said when the shocked neighbor brought me back. A lock was put on the screen door after that. According to Mother, I potty-trained myself in a "monkey-see, monkey-do" fashion. Mother says that at night I would stand in my crib and yell for Dad, "Hey, Joe, hat to potty!"

There are six kids in our family: Lili, Maggie, Lisa, Marshall, Lee, and Marie. The first five of us were born one right after another. Marie came nine years later. Most of my memories before the age of ten do not include my brothers and sisters. I have thought this to be rather odd, but perhaps not. Kids do tend to be rather self-involved that young. I remember places and have the knowledge and intelligence about events, but before my pre-teen years, there are very few memories that include my siblings. My memories of family, especially my brothers and sisters, hold a sense of rightness and delight rather than memories of events. I have many memories of my siblings once I was past the age of ten: road trips, co-babysitting, baseball games, singing my brothers awake, the attic affair. Many good solid memories. I even wrote a short little book about us for a college course. Even though I know we fought, as most siblings do, I really don't remember those parts of growing up. Well, there is one thing I remember—my siblings playing boom boom music on my behind whenever they got near! Drove me nuts, it did. Makes me smile now. My brothers and sisters are gifted with talents I admire. They sing, create art, sew, and write computer programs. For their gifts and their personalities, I am glad they are my family.

Early childhood memories are generally delightful. My fifth birthday stands out in my mind. We celebrated my fifth birthday in our backyard. I got to sit on top of the picnic table in a child-size blue lawn chair. A huge pink bow on the chair attested to its being a gift. Another gift that day was a loaf of French bread. I remember walking the perimeter of the backyard eating my bread and watching snails. It was a good day.

During the first several years of my life, we moved every time a baby was born. After the fifth child, we even changed states. I recall the next four years as being rather idyllic. We were surrounded by lots of family. I had many friends, including a best friend. Life was good.

Fourth grade was a year of wonder. Miss Ellie May Thatcher was my gifted and enthusiastic teacher. She taught me the love of learning and inspired my aspirations. This was the year I wrote a Christmas play, fell in love with Helen Keller, and learned to love reading. A fellow student introduced me to Laura Ingalls Wilder's Little House books. *On the Banks of Plum Creek* had me longing to be a prairie girl. Then there was the square dance jamboree. I felt privileged to dance with the tallest boy in the class. I adored square dancing. Yes, my ninth year was a very good year. I remember not only being a part of the world around me, but feeling connected to the world of my family and friends. It was a good life.

The October I turned ten, we moved across the country. I recall being enthusiastic about the move, looking forward to the adventure. We were having a house built. I chose blue and green as the colors for my bedroom. I do not recall being upset or worried in any way about this move. Yet, coinciding with the move, changes within my internal world began taking place. I began to feel isolated and friendless. I felt rejected by my peers. I felt that I had no best friend. My mind began to isolate itself. My sense of right and wrong became more rigid and began its tightening around my mind. False knowledge began to fill me with the pain of internal dark horribleness. I felt I was becoming that dark horribleness. I don't know what the difference was. I simply moved from feeling accepted to feeling tolerated. I was quiet, shy, smart, and desperately lonely. The loneliness sucked me right in.

Pretending played a key role during my childhood. I played extravagant soap opera games with my Barbie™ dolls into high school. Barbie™ dolls were the friends I felt at home with, the "lives" I could control. Barbie™ and Ken™ never fought. Their children, about thirteen of them, were beautiful and strong. Shoe boxes and doll cases became mansions of freedom.

At times, I couldn't tell the difference between dreams and real life. I remember an occasion of building spanking machines from three-foot two-by-fours with glistening sharp nails sticking out at one end. Several children lined up with their legs apart. The child to be spanked would crawl under their legs while being hit repeatedly with the two-by-fours and those damaging nails. Logic tells me this never happened and was merely a dream. Yet, for years, I couldn't decide if it really happened or not.

In some ways, pretend became my reality as an adult. Sometimes it is still difficult to differentiate between reality and thought or dreams. Magical thinking it has been called. If I think it, it will happen. If I think it, it is real.

Basically, I was a rule follower. Because of this, my brothers and sisters sometimes called me Queen Bee, especially when I tried to get them to follow the rules. (Being the eldest was not always easy!) It bothered me when rules weren't followed. It bothered me when I couldn't follow the rules. Later on, rules would become very important. I had to have them. They gave me boundaries when I had none. One of my students asked me if I had rules at my house. I thought about it and realized that rules were a part of how I survived, how I got through each day. Areas in my life where there were no set rules tended to be a bit out of whack. For example, there was no rule about hygiene other than a very itchy head told me I had better take a shower soon. Thank heaven my head itched a lot! If someone invited me to be somewhere at a certain time, I treated that time as a rule and there I was. This was the external world guiding my internal world for internally I was often in chaos. A part of me knew the world outside of me had an order my insides did not. That outside order became the rules and guidelines of my life.

At times so much unknown emotion dwelled within me that I became frozen. The emotion ached and fought to get out, but I just became frozen while all the feeling festered and boiled beneath the surface—sort of like a pimple before it comes to the surface, or the pain of a boil before it pops to release greenish stench-filled puss.

This was the beginning of my long bout with mental illness. And nobody knew it. I continued to laugh and smile. My grades in school were good. I had fun with my siblings and the kids in the neighborhood. It could be said that my life and I were quite normal. Yet, this was when the long term darkness began to build within me. It was a scary time of feeling friendless although our neighborhood had families bursting with children the right age, and I never lacked for playmates. The darkness found a small niche to hide in where it could slowly age, grow, and ferment, smelling like Limburger cheese or wine turned to vinegar. Not even I knew it was there. I knew I was lonely, but the loneliness did not show. I knew my head was filled with dark horribleness, but this, too, did not show. Everyone who knew me had the impression that I was sweet and cheerful, and probably a bit of a wimp. I was seldom able to stand my own ground on anything because I didn't know there was ground for me to stand on. I just went with the flow. I was a constant of smiles and giggles. Truthfully, this optimistic, cheerful, easygoing manner was not a façade. Unconsciously, I began living in two worlds—my external world of laughter and my internal world of misery. The battle in my head began in secret without my permission. My head wanted to go back to the way things used to be. Little did I know that a journey lasting more than thirty years had begun.

Two

After the move across country, life at home changed a bit. Due to some change in financial circumstances we never lived in that house that was being built. Extra stress came to fill our household and with it an increase in temper flare-ups that could be ugly and hurtful.

Mother is a delightful woman filled with laughter, people smarts, and kindness of heart. People love being around her. I love and admire her immensely. Mother was a room mother, a Bluebird leader, a doer. She is a woman of insight, laughter, and wisdom. But, I must let you know, Mother had a temper. Her temper could flare with the best of them, and after the move across country her temper took over with greater frequency and intensity. When Mother's temper took hold, her usual wisdom left her, and in its place came stress-related actions. Often words left her lips with frustrated rage, the words searing their painful way to sensitive ears. At these moments, the words spouting forth from Mother's lips were not only painful, they could be unkind. I cannot, even now share those words with you. I have blanked them out. On occasion, their memory can still make me sad. At my center, I cannot believe Mother meant her spiteful words and wrath — even when she took to spanking her cherubs. She was simply seeking the truth, and it wasn't always easy to find. Later, when we were grown and sitting around the kitchen table, a large framed picture suddenly fell off the wall and shattered. We all looked at it in surprise. Mother looked at it and said, "If I had come home and seen this when you were kids, I wouldn't have believed you." We all laughed. Truth had been spoken.

Mother, always an interesting mix of polar contrasts, could be the most delightful of people one minute and a raging torrent of word and action the next. When Mother was in a temper, we kids hoped for the phone to ring. "Lili, Maggie, Lisa, Marshall, and Lee! Get down here right this minute! *Someone* broke the vacuum cleaner. I want to know who did it and I want to know now!" Five faces looked as innocent as possible (Marie was too young to be guilty); every face wondered who the guilty party would be this time. "Who broke the vacuum cleaner? Speak up." Hearts pounding we'd all look at one another, daring each other to 'fess up. "Come on, tell the truth. Who broke the ...! And if we were lucky, the phone would ring. "Hello? ... Oh, hi, Cindy" (Said with relaxed lilting voice.) "What? You've got to be kidding. I can just see it!...Kids will be kids." Laughter and smiles filled Mother's voice. The tension relaxed. We kids were free for the moment.

I sometimes wondered at the swiftness of this change in temperament. How could her mood change so swiftly? The moments of Mother's temper could be very painful and hurtful. I don't think she liked herself during those moments, yet I don't think she knew how else to get her point heard. No, those moments of temper were not fun.

Having made this disclosure of Mother's temper, I need to reiterate that Mother loved us and raised us with a passion. While she would hold jobs outside the home, Mother was mostly a stay-at-home mom who sewed all our clothes, baby-sat neighbors' kids, and kept a fairly immaculate house. She loved being pregnant and lived in that state for many years. Mother was the center of our lives and did her best to remain that center.

It was sometimes hard to fathom Mother's conjoined passions of love and anger. It was not always easy to believe in her love for us. Yet, love us she did with her rather awing and consuming passion.

Mother's passion included her desire to know everything about her children, inside and outside. This part of Mother gave me feelings of claustrophobia. I was trying so hard to hide; she was trying so hard to know me. I felt like she was clawing at my core—sort of like in "Indiana Jones and the Temple of Doom" where one character stabs his finger into another character's chest and pulls out his beating heart. I know this was not Mother's intent. It was my growing darkness, my constant fear, and my need to hide.

Mother was disappointed that she was not my confidant. What she never understood or comprehended was that I confided in no one. I trusted no one. I could not allow myself to trust. What if people found out about my horribleness? At times I felt that Mother was pushing at me, begging for me, to confide in her. Something within me just wouldn't allow such sharing. I remember Mother frequently asking me, "Lili, what are you thinking?"

"Oh, nothing," I would truthfully reply.

"What do you mean nothing? You've got to be thinking about something." Mother could not fathom the idea that my mind often drifted off to the land of unconscious thought. She couldn't believe me when I told her I wasn't thinking of anything. Often, I felt like a liar though telling the truth. It got to the point where what I was thinking about was what to tell Mother when she asked me that dreaded question. My insides would squish together and try to hide even more.

During my teen years, Mother could fill me with angst and delight within moments of one another. How much of this was normal and how much was my internal darkness, I do not know. I admit to having had mixed feelings about Mother. Dark feelings existed within me twisted and gnarled with love and guilt and confusion. Sometimes my feelings were of the darkest black. At other times, I was filled with pure delight and joy. More recently, I have realized that much of the angst I held regarding my mother was due to Mother being a perfectionist. She wants everything to be just so, people and things alike. Somehow this most recent discovery and realization has freed me, for I am most definitely not a perfectionist. (And proud of it!) I am able to say, "Aah, that is her perfectionism kicking in," and usually delight in our differences.

Mother fills any room she enters with stories and laughter. She possesses an amazing store of wisdom and insight into people. She fought for and wanted us all to shine. She demands honesty and expects your best. She has high behavioral expectations for adults as well as for her children. At my graduation from junior high, Mother was appalled at the way parents were leaving the stands before the recessional was over. She wrote a letter to the local newspaper about the situation and how parents should show respect for our accomplishments. That letter was published annually for years. It filled me with pride. Still does.

Because of her great passion in loving us and disciplining us, Mother has been a most influential person in my life. Mother is awesome.

Mother is a talented woman who has never appreciated her own talents as much as she has been awed by the talents of others. Dad is one of the talents Mother holds in awe. He can talk to anybody about anything. He paints, writes, and has built furniture. Dad was made of a calmer, less flammable fabric than Mother. Nothing much seemed to bother him. Dad's workday had him leaving the house at 5:30 AM and returning home at 7:05 PM, leaving Mother home with the swarm of children. Still, Dad did his share of raising us. It was Dad who got us all tucked into bed. He let us play games such as "Let's Pull the Hairs on Daddy's Tum-Tum." On Friday nights, he made pancakes any color we desired. The boys often chose black or brownish gray or purple. I usually chose yellow.

My eighth grade birthday was pretty special. Mother was out of town for some reason and sent me flowers. I had never had flowers sent to me before! Dad took us kids to the circus. Before we could go to the circus, homework had to be finished. Sadly, I had more homework than time. Part of my homework was an English writing assignment. Dad helped out and wrote my story for me. He told me to get up early in the morning to copy it and to make changes in the story to make it mine. I changed the word "cigar" to "cigarette." The story got a B+. The B+ shocked my system. "Dad," I cried. "You are a writer. How could I get only a B+?" Dad just laughed at me and said he had written as if he were an eighth grader. I would rather have had an A, make that an A+.

Mother and Dad came from such different families that we often compared ourselves to one side or the other. I usually identified myself with the Warner side. It turns out I am a unique mix of Mother and Dad. Physically, I am most like my mother: same coloring, same size, similar health issues. Personality and interest wise, I am most like my dad with touches of Mother here and there. Though more laid-back like my dad, I have recently discovered that stress brings about a temper I did not know existed. Not as vibrant as Mother's, but it does exist. I admit that having a temper scares me. It reminds me of the dark potential within me. Like Mother, I am filled with laughter and humor. Like Dad, analyzing things is second nature. It is rather nice to know that features I admire in my parents are features within me; it is also nice to know I am my own person whole and separate from them. While it would be years before I would be able to appreciate who I am, I have always appreciated where I come from.

People often try to find the cause for the events of our lives, especially when it comes to mental illness. "Somebody had to have done something to you for you to have this mental illness." My mental illness was not a result of life at home. Life at home was sometimes fantastic, sometimes poopy, really poopy. While I believe that the harsh temper flare-ups at home had input into my emotional health, I do not believe they were the cause of my mental illness. No matter what came from Mother's anger toward us, I was always drawn to her laughter and devotion.

Mostly life at home was just life filled with smiles and laughter and joy, with a bit of turmoil and some icky stuff. The good times were really good. The bad times were really bad. They existed in tandem.

Three

It amazes me that my beginning spiral into darkness occurred unnoticed. Then again, there were all my smiles and laughter and joy. Of course there was happiness. Of course I had friends, and I generally appeared cheerful and content. But in the dark of my bedroom closet, sitting on a pile of dirty clothes, I hid the real me. I was lonely for the knowledge that one person would know all of my insides and still like me, no, love me.

There has always been a terror within me of people finding out about me. I want *somebody* to completely know me and still like me. The contradiction is obvious, yet both are true. Something horrible lurks within me waiting to be discovered by others. I do so well at hiding this darkness that even I have no clue as to its substance. It lurks behind, under, within every crevice of my being to the point of only me knowing that it, whatever *it* may be, exists. What would happen if the hidden horror became known? Others would despise me. I would become more tortured; my inside self would writhe in agony. There is something so dark and ugly that even Satan would turn away. The dank dungeon. Knowledge of its existence is enough torture. Oh, the vast destruction that would transpire should that horrible something ever come to light and be revealed. I don't know what it is, but it is always there. Always.

High school became another dichotomy of contrasts for me. I don't know that I can adequately share my experience. While I was part of a group of friends, I never felt a true belonging. I felt like an outsider. I felt that they had me as a friend for the convenience of it and that if we had not ridden the bus together daily, I would not have been chosen as a friend. This is the side of me that was filled with the knowledge that some horrible darkness existed within me. The world's reality was most likely different from my internal reality. I don't know.

It is not that I wasn't liked. I think I missed out because of my inability to share any of the secrets hidden within me—even with Janie, the person whom I thought of as my best friend. The struggling darkness of my internal world simply didn't allow for intimacy. On the other hand, there is much I don't know or remember.

There are good memories. Once Janie stood up in class and told the teacher, "No one gives Lili a 'D'!" (I have since reread the paper that received a 'D.' It was well earned.) I blushed constantly. My peers just had to look at me and the pink would flood my face. I was teased about my blushing daily. I think I enjoyed this attention, for I remember it with fondness. I remember lots of laughter. I remember Joey drinking huge glasses of lunch product that held anything the others put into it.

High school was often a mystery to me. I was never sure what to expect from others or myself. At the same time I got along with both the teachers and my peers. Overall, high school was probably okay. The only thing horrible was my internal ickiness. Darkness within me grew in spurts here and there throughout those four years.

Two of my friends, Sherry and Cherie, I greatly admired. Sherry was filled with creative exuberance. She was in all the school plays. Cherie had eyes that glittered with humor and joy. She had an aura of genteel ladylike behavior and reminded me of a southern belle. I wanted to be Sherry and Cherie.

I was a part-time member of the German Club and the Future Teachers of America Club. We lived far enough away from my high school that full-time participation in after school activities wasn't possible. During school, I helped a math teacher and worked in the school library. I loved working in the library. It made me feel important and special. Being an avid reader, I thrived on being surrounded by books and read whatever I could get my hands on. I especially loved reading Beanie Malone books by Lenora Mattingly Weber. Beanie was self-sufficient yet full of fret. I loved her world. I wanted her life.

In the library I also discovered the book that touched the core of my soul—and woke my thoughts of a spiritual nature. The book was *Christy* by Catherine Marshall. It was easy to relate to Christy and her thirst for life. It was easy to feel the love the children had for her. I wanted their love. I believed in their love. And once again I wanted to be someone other than myself. I wanted to be Christy.

For most of my four high school years I held a major crush on one particular boy. He and I were friends at church, but I didn't exist for him at school. He had the most gorgeous twinkly brown eyes.

I tutored another boy in German and chemistry. We got along pretty well. He walked me to class with an arm around my waist, but when I sold flowers for Flower Day, he bought flowers for another girl. My waist felt betrayed.

Whenever I was free from duties and homework, I rode my bike. It was a one speed and a lot of work to ride. I longed for peace of mind and riding my bike helped. Round and round the block I would go. Pedaling, always pedaling. I longed to be noticed. I would ride my bike hoping to catch glimpses of certain boys, hoping they would catch glimpses of me. The energy of my horribleness kept those pedals going. Thoughts flew through my brain, all sorts of thoughts. Boys. Fears. Yearnings. I pedaled for relief. I pedaled for freedom from myself. The great energy I expended on these bike rides granted some relief from the internal confusion of my mind.

My other occupation when free-time came my way was the piano. I took lessons for eleven years. I loved the emotion of classical music. I loved pounding the keys with Concone's "Anxiety." Fast and furious my fingers would fly. The music became an extension of the havoc within me. My piano teacher convinced me to give a solo recital. She didn't, however, want me to play from memory. I rebelled in an unnoticeable quiet way. I opened the music to the wrong page. The boy who was my page turner became quite puzzled as he couldn't find where I was. I finally whispered to him to just turn the page once in awhile. He did. I made my piano teacher happy by using the music books. I made myself happy by playing from memory.

I wanted to be a great pianist. Interestingly, my need to follow the rules affected my ability to excel at piano. I was never able to play anything other than classical-style music. Four-four time. Three-four time. Steady beat, steady rhythm. I had to have defined confines—even in my piano music.

Senior year was a struggle. I felt less and less a part of my peers. My friends appeared to be finding and discovering lives of their own. I found it difficult to be a participant in many senior activities. I felt isolated in the midst of my friends and therefore was minimally involved. I even managed to receive a couple "you-could-fail-this-class" notices. (Have no fear, I got Bs.) It just felt as though I was being left behind.

In reality, I was preparing for college, working part-time and being inducted into the National Honor Society. I went to football and basketball games. People wrote nice things in my yearbook. To the eyes of others, nothing appeared to be out of order. This must be when I began pretending. Pretending to be cheerful, to be happy, to be unaffected by disappointment.

The one truly painful event in high school was prom. I didn't go. I wasn't invited. One of my friends told me a certain boy had a crush on me and would ask me to the prom. He asked her instead. I felt betrayed. Prom night had me in my bedroom watching as he picked my friend up next door in his father's car and drove off into the sunset. That painful moment fed my insecurities and loneliness. Pretending became increasingly more important.

During high school, my writing focus was journaling. Late at night I would be in the closet or under the covers with a flashlight writing furiously. My journals were filled with dark anguished thoughts; some thoughts related to the world around me, most related to the world within me. At the end of high school, I took all my journals and shredded them into the cafeteria trash barrels. Fear of being discovered brought this about. My journals were filled with thoughts I dared not let anyone know. Thoughts I begged for someone to know.

Lili stood by the trash barrel in the noisy, indifferent cafeteria and ripped up her journals. All of them. Page by page she shredded the depths of her soul. This page cried out with its words of pain. That page dark with angry penciled letters. Another with fear.

Fear was the worst. How could Lili have written such vicious, fearful words? She didn't remember writing all of them, but because of those words, Lili knew she had to destroy her journals. All of them. What if people ever read them?

Tears welled up threatening to spill over onto the pages she shredded. Sadness threatened to keep these words that had poured from her soul. Fear kept her shredding. Every page must disappear as if it had never existed. No one must ever know the truth of how ugly she, Lili, truly was.

Lili had chosen the cafeteria for the anonymity it afforded. Granted many of its occupants knew her, but their very presence added to Lili's feeling of being unknown. She was an invisible presence, unnoticed and hidden. Lili was the forgotten picture on the wall—comfortably visible, seldom looked at. She felt safe there. The people were blind to anything not immediately in their world.

A few more pages before relief could occur. Or would there be relief. How can one feel relief at destroying the contents of her soul?

With the final page Lili let out a sigh. The deed was done. Her secrets of emotion were no longer in danger of discovery. Lili thought of setting the thing on fire, but vetoed that idea. Anonymity and setting fire to a cafeteria trash barrel did not reach an accord. Somebody would be certain to notice.

Inside my head, all my journals were burned in that high school trash barrel. That is what my head sees even now. Logic would say that I did not have a bonfire going in the school cafeteria. My head says something else. (I often refer to my head instead of my mind because many thoughts did not and do not seem a part of my brain and mind but are somehow in my head separate from me.)

As high school passed into college and early adulthood, there continued to be bouts of hidden depression and a phobia of what people thought of me. I was certain everyone was talking about me and my terribleness. I was sure my name and deeds would be found in their journals. I knew everyone ignored me because of that ugly horribleness within me. The terror inside my being drove me to search through my college roommate's notebooks and journals to discover what she was saying about me. I never could find such writings. I determined they were well-hidden or in storage. It never occurred to me that my roommate was *not* writing about me. I mean, why weren't we, my horribleness and I, the focus of her life? I was aching to be noticed.

It was not about being a narcissistic egomaniac. It was about the search for myself. Even back then I was convinced everyone knew all about me and my terrible, horrible darkness while I knew nothing of me.

The loneliness I feel within the depths of my soul cannot be described using any words of a mere mortal person. Silence crashes against my ears with a force equal to that of any ocean wave. Harsh and painful, the spikes of loneliness stab away at me, piercing down to the bone a guard I have nurtured so carefully with every breath in which my lungs have indulged. Erosion has destroyed my spine and stolen my stamina. Instead, my body and soul are filled with heavy sand. Gravity pulls my weight down steadily until I am no longer on top of the world, but have entered the black and mysterious caves of depression. The caves of depression are frightening because as of yet they are uncharted. No one above has discovered all the nooks and crannies. Most are even unaware that there truly is such a cave. The blackness surrounds me. I scream incessantly for someone to come to my rescue. Nobody does. It is not that people do not care. Though black and so thoroughly suffocating, the cave is invisible to the naked eye. High tide continues its efforts at destruction. My ears throb from the pain of it all. "Help me! HELP ME!" I scream and my brain becomes hoarse. So tired. I am so tired. The tide ebbs out, and I can open my eyes. Once again there is sunshine for a little while. My hand held up in the light makes funny little shadows on the wall. It turns back and forth as if to prove it is really there. Slowly, my hand comes to my face. I touch my cheeks and lips with a lightness that tickles. I can feel the tickle. I can see the sunshine. An inspection of my surroundings proves that the cave has disappeared for now. Long, deep, and painful breaths lower my tense muscles into a state of complete relaxation. My body is limp. For now, and for at least a bit of the future, I know that I am safe from the uncharted depths of that black, dark cave.

People come and go. Friends, relatives, and strangers smile as they pass by never knowing or suspecting the cave through which I have just traveled. My ears continue to throb from the silence. I find a radio to fill the space with sound. The silence in my ears diminishes slowly until an equilibrium has been achieved. All is not right with the world, but it is livable. I wash my hair. Life continues and so must I.

College was pretty nondescript. It came. It went. I watched for people watching me. I searched for those journals talking about me. College pretty much just happened.

I attended a junior college for two years. It was cheap and near home. During these two years, I spent my time craving human contact of the male kind. I would sit in the cafeteria watching and waiting. Would anyone recognize me? Would anyone stop by and talk to me? Would I be able to hide? The agony between wanting to be noticed and dying to hide filled me with constant tension. I didn't get great grades. I was too busy fighting myself and hungering to fit in.

For the second two years, I changed colleges. Having always loved children, becoming a teacher seemed like a natural step to take. During my teens, little kids would come knocking at our door asking if I could come out and play. I paid for my first two years of college with baby-sitting money. At fifty cents an hour, that was a lot of baby-sitting! I chose to major in special education, specifically visual impairments. Thankfully, the cheapest university in the state had a respected program in this very field. I had always thought I wanted to be Helen Keller, but it turned out that I sought to be Annie Sullivan, Helen's teacher and companion. My yearning was about being drawn to people in need—people, especially children, who might need me. There was always that flicker of hope that someone just might need me. What a concept. What a dream.

For some reason, I could now focus on course work and managed to graduate with honors. I enjoyed the challenge of learning braille and getting around with a blindfold on. I somehow felt more normal with the blindfold. Perhaps it was that the internal darkness enjoyed meeting up with the external darkness.

Working in the dorm's food service was my safe haven. I loved it. I felt comfortable and confident in this environment. Most of the staff members were in their sixties, and we were best of friends. They gave me a burnt orange hand-blown glass dove when I graduated. Working in food service was the joyous part of college.

My first job out of college proved to be fairly boring. I loved the children I worked with, but they weren't enough to fill my ever growing internal hole. The small town was far from crowds, which was a relief of sorts, fewer people to deal with or be suspicious of. I liked the romanticism of living in a small town. I enjoyed the slower pace. I enjoyed being able to walk everywhere. A recurring dream of mine has me living in a small town in a one and a half room "house" where the bedroom is a raised crawl space behind the one and a half rooms and is not easy to see or get into. A rather safe place. I like it. Life in this small town, while enjoyable, was not a cure for what ailed me. My mind went into overtime with loneliness, fear, and writing about a fly getting drunk from the leftover wine in my wine glass.

For a while, I lived in a house with two friends. Whenever someone knocked on the door, I would hide in a corner away from the window in hope that they'd go away. I was sure the intruders would want something from me I couldn't give. People at the door scared me. I was afraid they would discover me and wouldn't leave me alone. I *always* hid from the Jehovah Witnesses and Mormons. They scared me the most. What if they could see inside me and see that vast darkness of mine? I couldn't chance it, so I hid.

One of my roommates asked me to go to the movies with her to see "American Gigolo." In my naiveté, I agreed to go with the excitement I always felt when a musical was around. Little did I know that there were two definitions to the word "gigolo". Imagine my shock when instead of gigolos dancing and singing their hearts out, Richard Gere stood naked in front of my very own eyes. My, my, my. The roommate sniggered and smiled a knowing smile. Both the movie and her silent teasing hurt. I was angry. I never let Roomie know I was angry. The anger just slid into my darkness to fester. And while the anger festered, my laughter abounded. I laughed with Roomie about the misadventure. Trust became more difficult.

This first teaching experience of mine came to an end when my good friend, Bailey, and I decided to quit boredom and seek adventure. We chose a fishing lodge in Alaska. Bailey's parents wanted to know if we were headed into a drug ring. My dad wanted to know how I knew it wasn't white slavery. Since Bailey and I had found the job through a U.S. government listing of summer jobs, I told Dad that if I didn't show up in October, which was when the job ended, he should give Jimmy Carter a call. Jimmy Carter was, after all, in charge of the United States government.

Our jobs in Alaska were at a small, ritzy fishing lodge on a lake at the north end of the Kenai Peninsula. Bailey and I were maids cleaning guest rooms in the morning, chef's assistants in the afternoon, and hostesses during the cocktail hour before dinner. What an awesome experience!

Bailey's friendship would become lost to me in Alaska. For some unknown, pressure-filled reason, my internal world leaked its way into my external world. Bailey had done nothing wrong, yet I began to feel she would latch onto me and never let go. I began feeling claustrophobic and had to flee. I did my best to avoid her. In reality, I was probably avoiding myself. Bailey hadn't a clue about what was going on, so she found a new set of friends. It was impossible for me to explain to Bailey what was going on. For one thing, I didn't know myself. I wish I could apologize to her.

Four

That first summer I had a major crush on one of the chefs. This particular chef happened to be a tormented soul. Our rooms were connected by a bathroom. On occasion, late at night, the chef and I would sit in the bathroom discussing the torments and lamentations of his life. It was quite the party. After our adventure in Alaska, I never heard from him again. This was probably a good thing considering my own darkness. I did put together a book for him on friendship. It came back marked "addressee unknown."

One of the most delightful times in my twenties occurred during a six-month stint on the East Coast between summers in Alaska. I worked in an ice cream restaurant as dishwasher, ceiling cleaner, short order cook, and waitress. The crew and I had a blast.

Bo, Slim and I would sing television theme songs together. Our best were the themes from "Green Acres" and "Mr. Ed". At the top of our lungs we would wail "Green acres is the place to be ...." One evening, I invited my coworkers over for homemade pizza. The yeast I used must have been extremely fresh for the dough kept rising and rising. I ended up with fifteen pizzas rather than three. I almost ran out of pans. The evening was a success; everyone was required to take at least one pizza home.

My married boss had a bit of a crush on me. Thankfully he never behaved inappropriately. He gave me flowers when I left with a card I keep in my wallet. It says, "You are very special. Best of luck always."

Bo and I clicked with friendship. He was a senior in high school, so some people teased us about our friendship. Although I was in my mid-twenties, I was closer to Bo's age socially and emotionally. We played like children taking field trips. Just before I left, we jokingly had our "big date." The goal was to have a drink with an umbrella in it. We went to a Chinese restaurant and ordered pineapple juice with umbrellas. Not only did we get the umbrellas, our juice was served in pineapples with a straw. I loved the people I worked with.

Away from work and my coworkers, the darkness in my head would return, and I would pretend that all was right with my world. At work, I felt free and accepted as never before. I hated to leave the East Coast when my time was up, yet knew I couldn't stay. I was committed to returning to Alaska for another season. The gang made an incredible fun audio tape for me after I left. I still listen to it on occasion. It represents a period of time I felt relatively loved.

After my second summer in Alaska, I traveled the country by bus for a while. It was a journey of youth seeking excitement and of me looking for my proper place in the world. I visited various cooking schools, Disney World, and friends. When my travels ended, I found myself living with my dad's mother. Grandma M. can only be described as the epitome of goodness and kindness. Relatively reserved most of the time, she let herself "go nuts" when watching sports. I once came home and found Grandma listening to three football games at once. She had brought the kitchen radio into the living room to listen to one game while she flipped back and forth between two other games on television. I can see her now, clapping her hands and shouting, "Go, go go!"

Grandma M. and I had a delightful time together. We played our own ongoing version of Yahtzee with scores reaching the 100,000s. We laughed at the silly events in my life, like the time I decided to condition my hair with Vaseline, or the time my car got stuck in a hole of ice in the alley at two in the morning. Grandma M's house was a haven of safety. Her total acceptance of everyone, combined with her gentle spirit, allowed me to feel a certain internal calmness I had never experienced before. Some of my darkness became less frightening. I knew her house held love and I knew some of that love was for me.

From the time the darkness and worry about my terribleness began to torture my mind, my most consuming desire became a suffocating need to be loved. Know me; love me. Please. It was an enormously lonely and never-ending place to be. Love seemed far away in a place untouchable, unseeable, and with little hope. At the same time, I was sure that people would want something from me I couldn't give. I couldn't trust any of them.

In my head, I knew people loved me. There were times when I could feel their love. Time with my family was filled with laughter and board games and music. I had many male friends with whom I had great fun and with whom I corresponded. Some of these friendships were very special. Life itself was normal and okay. It was my head that kept going off on its own little trips.

Five

In my late twenties, I loved to cook and was headed to a top culinary institute on the east coast when I made a stop along the way. I left Grandma M's for cooking school with little money and no means of support. I figured things would work themselves out once I arrived. I never made it. Midwest, USA called and I answered.

One day I took a walk around the local university. On a wall in the education building was posted a bright blue piece of paper. The piece of paper yelled at me, literally, to take it. I tried several times to walk past that blasted blue piece paper, but it just kept screaming at me. I don't remember the words. I do remember the screaming noise. With every step I took trying to get past that hanging blue piece of paper, the screaming grew louder. It was obnoxious, irritating, embarrassing. Finally, I gave up and snatched the sheet of paper off the wall. Immediately, the screaming noise stopped. I cast furtive looks around, tucked the piece of paper under my arm, and scampered back to the motel terrified that someone had seen me. For some reason, the fact that the paper yelled at me didn't bother me. It didn't even seem weird. I was, however, worried that someone was going to yell at me for taking the blue sheet of paper off the wall. When I managed to get into the motel room, I glanced at that sheet of paper, readying to toss it in the trash. Something about it caught my eye, so I read it. That screaming piece of blue paper turned out to be a flyer for a graduate program in special education. The deadline for application was long overdue. I applied anyway.

For a month or so, I lived in a motel. I had been holed up in the motel room for several days when the motel manager offered me a job as maid. I took the job. A few months later, I was offered a spot in the graduate program.

My mind was filled with the joy a job and school could offer me. Maybe this was where I would finally fulfill that desperate need for love. Maybe here the darkness would go away.

Surprisingly, in the midst of this joy, I had dangerous "dreams." Orange and yellow M&Ms were mixed in with sleek silver bullets. A gun just glittered amid the M&Ms. I kept wanting to use the bullets and the gun, but could never find them even though I knew they were on the night stand. More than one version of this dream occurred:

There is a gun on the table before me. The barrel glitters. Sunshine pours through the window, pinpointing its light on the table beside the bed where I lay. Mahogany wood. Glazed silver. The one bullet shines like a star in the pitch of night. Too bad the bullet will not fit the gun. The gun is not real. It is only a prop. A cap gun. I have been alone all my life. My family surrounds me with a love I cannot feel. I was born laughing. I still laugh. I was also born incapable of accepting love. My heart yearns and aches to be held. My psyche, or whatever, hides in a pit. Sometimes I feel as if my entire being is turned inside out and that is why I have these feelings. What feelings? I am filled to the brim with feelings and have no outlet. Perhaps I just do not allow myself an outlet. I don't know. I do not know a lot of things. I picture myself inside out. Black in the middle. Red on the outside. Just a squiggly mass of blubber. No direction. No place to go. No accomplishments. This all sounds so morbid. It is, I guess. Death, dying. I always see myself without a body of bones. All I see in death is my skull. The black eye holes. The teeth hanging in a wicked grin. Sneering at me. I try to close my eyes to the picture. This proves to be impossible because the picture I see is in my eyes, a part of them. My brain has implanted the image of death into my eyelids. No matter where I look, the skull lurks about somewhere, never far away. Sometimes there are worms and spiders in the skull. When there are, I can't seem to get rid of them either. Worms, spiders, and the skull. Every nook and cranny of my life is filled with them. A brown prescription bottle of Motrin rests next to the gun. It is filled with big orange pills. If I take the entire bottle, there should be enough of something in them to get rid of the skull in my mind's eye. Sometimes I think of what a car crash would feel like. Should I run into that tree? How fast can I get the car to go before I run into that cement building? Just little thoughts like that. I fear using scissors. Sometimes the points look so inviting. I depress the point slightly against the base of my throat. My heart beats so hard I can feel slight vibrations through the scissors. I stare at my hand in wonder. Could I ever really use these to end it all? To kill myself sounds so definite, so final. Gently the blades glide across my wrists. I don't bother cutting because I heard somewhere that if you slash your wrists, you have to hold them under water in order to bleed to death. Who wants to bleed to death anyway? Why drag out the end? I would rather die quickly. I want to know when I end. Or do I? I … People always used to admire the constant smile on my face. I wonder where it went. I don't know. I know nothing. My favorite candy is M&Ms. Motrin probably doesn't taste like M&Ms. What happens if I die and then find out that there is nothing but dirt and worms. As the childhood song went, "The worms crawl in the worms crawl out, the worms play pinochle on my snout." What if it is real?

Mostly, I was able to shove this dream aside and focus on the adventure of grad school. I felt challenged and safe at school. It was a place where I knew success was possible. School always gave me hope.

The graduate program was a strenuous one. We fellows, as we were called, taught from 8 a.m. to 4 p.m., attended classes from six until ten, and did eight hours of research assistance work each week. I had to quit my job at the motel because there was no time for it. Thankfully, I received a small stipend to live on. Again, I was living in a smallish town and was enjoying the lifestyle. I lived in a converted garage having a kitchen, bathroom and one large living/sleeping space. For a while, I had a part-time roommate. We got along rather well. Only one thing went wrong. She touched my table. This table was my sacred place, holding all my secrets. My journals and other private writings were kept there. Sandy had asked if she could rearrange the furniture. I said, "Just don't touch my table." Sandy touched my table. She moved it across the room, from east to west, and I freaked out. My heart panicked and I exploded in fear. With clenched teeth and fists I paced rapidly up and down the room. Visions of red filled my mind's eye. My heart raced. My palms sweated. All my secrets had been invaded! I was terrified. What had she seen? Had knowledge of my horribleness leaked out? Did she now know? Sandy wasn't home. Anger welled up joining the fear. How dare she touch my table! How dare she touch my secrets! I grabbed paper and felt tip pen and scribbled a note meant to strike terror. I wrote that even Princess Diana would not be allowed to touch my table! This veiled threat must have worked for Sandy hid from me at a friend's house. I apologized for my note, and life went on. Still, she did move my table. (Do I ever let go of these things?)

As life went on I bounced back and forth between more sane and less sane, more depressed and less depressed. Joy in life, despair fighting life. And no one knew. For I was Lili Marie Warner, the girl who was always seen laughing, smiling, and quite cheerful. What an actress.

Six

Life at thirty seemed to be on the upswing. After finishing school, I moved across the country. I was given the honor of teaching children with special needs. I found a church I liked and joined the singles group. Friendship now seemed possible. I truly loved this period of time. People in my life. A job I enjoyed.

Enter a friend of the opposite sex, XY. (His name is Weston, but for my own sanity I shall refer to him as XY. You are welcome to call him by name.) When I met XY, I knew immediately and with every ounce of conviction within me that this would be my most important friendship. It turned out to be life-changing.

Relationships with boys and men throughout my life have felt unique. I often seemed to be the springboard for males. They befriended me, and had jolly times with me, readying themselves to leap into the relationship with their true love. It usually did not bother me when my male friends married someone else. Being dropped as a friend once they married — that bothered me. Cold. It felt cold. I no longer received letters. I no longer had a friend. The lack of letters and relationships caused great sadness in my heart. As the letters dwindled, my head developed more games to play that fed into my core beliefs about myself. Beliefs of being unlovable. Beliefs of that deep, dark horribleness keeping people away.

When XY came onto the scene, I was ripe for a new horizon. I grew to believe in the possibility of someone discovering they loved me and XY was to be that someone. I put my whole being on the line; I poured myself into becoming part of what I would later call "our nonrelationship." Other interludes of nonrelationships had danced through my life. A marriage proposal once invited me to believe, but it was merely the admiration of a tipsy boy. I have received flowers from a married man and was once told I was passion waiting to be explored. Ah, the dreams.

Often I would remember things, and people would tell me I was wrong. For example, in my early teens, I remember being chased with knives. Round and round we ran in a circle, knives glistening with wicked laughter at my back. For years, I would jump and scream if I dropped a knife. I came to laugh about this incident. The years had turned it funny rather than terrifying. Finally I was told it had never happened. Disbelief and anger filled me. At times, doubt still fills me. My mind believes in the incident; it still sees those glistening blades.

Though I can't give examples, other incidents exist. Such and such never happened some would say. So and so doesn't remember doing that. It was confusing. I couldn't be inventing all of it. So, throughout my friendship with XY, I would write down every event and important word. I set out to prove I was right. I would attempt to prove that my reality was the same as that of someone else.

XY and I attended different churches but the same singles group. We were both a bit shy, yet outgoing and involved in all the singles group activities. We sang in an a capella Christmas choir, went white water rafting, and just had a good time.

After a few years of group fun, XY made a move. XY called me. The phone conversation held many long bits of silence as we worked through our shyness and newness at conversing with one another. With this first phone call, my journey into both the brightest and darkest of days began.

XY and I became best of friends. We talked on the phone for hours, often playing word games with the dictionary. We talked daily and went on outings. It was a friendship of delight, filled with laughter. And, as mentioned earlier, I didn't trust my mind. I wrote everything we did on a calendar. Every little event, every talk, I wrote down. I didn't want anybody to tell me I was wrong or that things I remembered hadn't happened. It was a good calendar filled with the fun XY and I had. It was a time of joy and wonder.

There is much to be said for pure friendship. There is much to be said for the destruction of such a friendship. I did a good job aiding in the destruction of this beautiful friendship. I presumed this friendship was the one for forever. I wanted it to be forever. But, even in the midst of joy and goodness, my head played games with me.

Major change in our friendship came. I thought we were dating. I also fell in love. I wanted XY to hold my hand. I knew he was shy and reserved. I wasn't longing for his kiss (at least not most of the time!) I simply wanted XY to hold my hand. Holding my hand would prove he cared. Holding my hand would prove me lovable.

It turned out XY didn't want to hold my hand. He began a dance of avoidance. I went crazy with my strangling hope. Weren't we dating? Weren't we? We constantly did things together. My train of thought made sense to me. XY felt my strangling hope and told me that not only were we not dating, but that I was too fat for him ever to think of me in "that way". Those were the most horrific and hurtful words I had ever heard.

> I bought this book because I liked the cover. "A Woman's Journal." I like that. I have never had sex. I wish that just once someone would want to have sex with me. Why, if I believe in abstinence without marriage, do I want someone to want me? What is wrong with me? I am a good, funny, intelligent person. I am not thin, but I am not ugly either. Though I feel ugly these days. I feel ugly inside myself. Anger, sadness and lots of pain. I want to go up to XY and yell my head off. I want to scream and pound my fists, against his chest. I want to yell "HOW DARE YOU!" You see, XY has turned out to be the cruelest of them all. In his efforts not to hurt me, he has destroyed me. Not only did XY dump me, he ripped away and stole all my memories. It is one thing to be dumped. It is quite another to be told that the good part never was. I don't want my birthday this year because last year's never existed. It was all a fake. WHAT IS TRUE? XY doesn't want me. I hate that. Why can't somebody want me? Why doesn't XY want me? I want to be wanted; I need to be wanted. More than that right now I need to know what was true. WHAT WAS TRUE? What really went on? Do I know? And is it different from what I wrote? Am I being honest? Why can't I just scream at the top of my lungs and be done with it, feel real and whole again? Why am I falling apart? SCREAM, SCREAM, SCREAM ... Last night I dreamed I drove my car straight into a red brick wall. What does this mean?

My confused mind went ballistic as if all the Independence Day fireworks exploded at once. Ironically, XY was declaring his independence from me. My calendar became my armor. "Look," I screamed into the silence of my phone, "look at all I have written. See? I wrote it all down. I didn't make it up. We did go out. We did. You cared for me. I can prove it. You gave me gifts with meaning. It wasn't a lie. It wasn't. I didn't make it up, did I?"

The emotional turmoil worked its way up to a hurricane status! My behavior became that of a beggar pleading for his affection. I wrote up contracts to give us roles and rules to follow. I walked and drove around town searching, determined to run accidentally into XY. I longed for his love. Desperation consumed my every waking moment. I *had* to be loved, damn it. I had to be known. I had to hang onto XY. He was the one to love me. He was. But, there were facts to face. XY knew me and did not want me. He refused to love me. He proved to me that my calendar was a lie and that my deepest fear had come true. I was not lovable. I was not wanted. I was tolerated. Stacked against all other disappointing relationships, this was the one that killed me. As the days and weeks went by, I fell apart piece by piece.

In the end, reality of the friendship with XY proved to be part real, part fantasy, part screaming desire. The ending of the friendship proved to be the unbalancing act of my brain. I grabbed at all the straws I could find only to have them crushed one by one. Sometimes by XY in his aloofness or the cruelty of his denials. Usually by myself in my destructive desperation. I slid down the slide only to land in a pile of muck that would grow stickier and deeper with time. Ever seen and smelled the muck of a hog farm? That was my life.

Seven

My best pal had declared independence from me, and I responded by discovering that I had no self. Tears became my constant companion. The fetal position became my mode of being at home. A baby bottle became my water glass. Once again the desperation of loneliness sucked the energy and life out of me. This time it was worse. Tentacles of darkness engulfed me. Insanity became the point toward which I was headed. I was sure of it. In my head, I no longer existed.

At first, I attempted to remain a part of the singles group. Sadly, each and every event dragged me further into that downward spiral of being a nothing, of feeling utterly empty and completely alone. Being with XY and friends caused my pain to increase exponentially. All my social yearnings were destroying me. Such pain. I didn't want to break away from the group, but in the end survival mode took over and I left. I didn't even know I had a survival mode. I was too busy drowning to notice. Even now I cannot fathom the invisible strength that led to that lifesaving decision. My only explanation is God. It had to have been God who granted me the strength to break away. As much as I enjoyed being a part of that group, I knew I would not survive if I remained. What an agonizing decision. What a necessary decision. What already felt like a barren life was now the bleakest of deserts without even a mirage for hope. This was when I began living in my bedroom, the smallest room in the house.

Daily my self-esteem swirled down that whirlpool of draining water until I no longer existed at all. I was nothing, nada, zip. My body made its physical journey from place to place, and most people could not tell that I was missing. If ever there was a legendary actress of wholeness, it was I. No one knew I cried every night for hours at a time.

No one knew I locked all the windows and doors and turned off the phone for days at a time. No one knew I lived in my bedroom for eight years and ate only toast and milk for at least two of those years. Smallest room in the house, yet it had everything I required for survival except the toilet and the refrigerator. No one knew all this. No one would have guessed. No one knew for I couldn't and wouldn't let them know. There is so much more people will never know. I don't even know it all, yet my body and mind survived it.

It is truly strange not to have a sense of being a self. I am not certain  I can describe it with any skill or clarity. There was a body, and a series of physical and mental activities accomplished each day, but there was no attachment to identity. In the movie "Run Away Bride" the bride character took on the likes and dislikes of her many grooms. The bride eventually searched for her own identity. She had to know herself in order to love and be loved. I, however, was in no shape to search for my own identity. Monstrous waves of emotion were crowding in, taking over my mind.

The tears had become nonstop. Every minute of every day was consumed with the thoughts and fears of XY. Lili still couldn't believe the cruelty, the betrayal of XY. He didn't love her. He said she was too fat for him to love. Okay, so he didn't say those exact words. XY never used exact words. XY infamously filled airspace with euphemistic language. Euphemistically cruel. Cruelly euphemistic? "You don't fit the body type that I will ever be attracted to." It would have felt better if he had just said, "You are fat. I don't like fat." But, no, XY danced around the table on his hands rather than standing on his feet. I hate XY. Lili understood for the first time what it meant not to know who she was. She became nothing when all she believed to be true was stolen from her heart and her head. The result was more confusion than she had ever felt in her entire life, and that was much confusion. Lili began having visions of driving straight into signs or trees or buildings. She decided to drive up to Flagstaff and drive off a cliff.

Tears ran my life. Minimal control of them existed. I held only the briefest of interactions with people because I had to escape for more tear flowing.

My life was a lie, a gigantic façade. I pretended everything. Every emotion was intense, overwhelming and indefinable. I wasn't just depressed. I was in a dank, dark cavern beneath the surface of the earth falling further and further toward the earth's molten core. My view of life lay beneath the darkest sky on the longest night, flashing between subzero and boiling. Fear does not begin to describe the terror I felt at being lost and at being unable to find myself. Panic and discomfort were merely surface scratches festering in wait for the future.

A voice began speaking to me about death. I feared being in public where people had expectations of me.

"Hi, Lili! How ya doin'?" Terror strikes my heart at the sound of these words. My heart becomes frozen; my breathing is put on hold. My mind races in ferocious fear. How am I?? Adrenaline pumps faster and faster. My sweaty palms receive fingernail dents from my clenched fists. I feel ready to explode with the swirling answers. I want to kill myself. I want to scratch my face into bloody shreds. I hate life and the world. Do you really want to know how I am? I can't find my shoes. I think someone stole them so I have to wear my snow boots. They're the only footwear I can find. I might lose my job because, well, I don't know why. You want to know how I am? I DON'T EVEN KNOW WHO I AM, so how do I tell you how I am!

People spoke the most harmless words. They thought they were being polite. I knew they were trying to catch me. Those damn people waited for that easy response. I never knew what to say. I never knew what they wanted of me. "I'm fine, and you?" Ha. I wasn't fine and could care less how they were faring. How does one answer "how are you" when the world is confusing and seemingly mixed up? And that's just the beginning. I often wondered why the world wouldn't slow down so I could get my bearings again. There was just too much. Too much noise. Too much color. Too many voices. Too much feeling. Too much of everything. Except love. There was too little love. And where the heck were my shoes?

I think my need for love completely surpassed everyone else's. I craved love. There was a desperateness in this need that wore others out and kept me empty. I knew people loved me. The knowledge was in my head, but I didn't feel it. The rage, fear and anger—and that black hole of depression— were so completely consuming in their battle for dominance and recognition that sweet gentle love hadn't much of a chance. The battle of overwhelming emotion carved out a cavernous hole seemingly empty of love, but filled with loneliness. A black, dank, ravenous loneliness had little hope in recognizing and feeling the love I craved.

To be understood was one of the deepest desires in Lili's own soul. How she longed for just one person to understand her inside and out. But that wasn't all. Lili wanted not only to be understood, she wanted to be loved. Hollow. That was how Lili felt. Where was that one mystical person who would understand her, know her, and still love her? Lili felt the downward spiral begin. Down, down, down, she went. Why doesn't anybody love me. God, what is your plan? It can't be too much if you keep me down here squashed and helpless. Her spirit slowly shrank, shriveling like a grape drying in the sun. Being understood drifted further into the distance. Being loved became an impossibility. Lili slid down in her chair, arms crossed. She became invisible to others, disappearing into her own fears and black hollow of existence. Nothing mattered. No one else existed. Lili herself no longer existed. Lili now found herself in a silent torturous black abyss. Death would be a step up.

After six months of never-ending tears, I sought therapy. During a surprisingly lucid moment, I discovered I needed help. It suddenly occurred to me that people shouldn't spend their life in tears, and evidently my tear ducts were not going to dry up.

Hence the long journey began.

The Road Down the Path

Find rest, O my soul, in God alone;
my hope comes from him.

Psalm 62:5

Eight

$\mathscr{H}$ arry was a nice enough guy. He was also a good therapist. I just threw him for a loop. After the first session Harry felt we probably needed to meet only every other week. He was most likely under the illusion that I was simply distraught over the end of my nonrelationship with XY. Harry suggested that I journal during the week and bring my writings next time.

Leave me alone. Everything. Everybody. Just stop it!! Aaaaaaah …

When I wake up in the morning, I am surprised. Always. How could I wake up when I am certain that sleep won't come? Yet, every night, *every* night, solid coma-like sleep comes somehow. My insides may be in shambles, my mind so horribly confused, yet still I sleep and then awaken.

I feel—isolated—as if I am here but not really. I know mentally that if I were to walk up to somebody and strike up a conversation they would respond. But emotionally, I cannot do it. I know I would just stand there and never say a word. My confidence seems to come and go in spurts.

If people *love* me, why do they also run from me? Or demand things from me?

Pearl Harbor. World wide hunger. The homeless. The students I work with. They all give me reason for guilt. So what if I am dumped as a friend for no reason over and over. So what if XY was the best person ever to enter my life and bring to surface more pain and hurt than I ever knew possible to exist in one body, mind and spirit. So what. Why doesn't my thankfulness and belief carry me beyond the importance of myself? Why do I have this need to become whole? Why do I feel my personal pain has more importance and strength than the pain of the world?

And why won't the pain go away? Why won't the anger go away, and why don't you tell me how to get rid of it all?

I want to be the me who cared for others. I am tired of being the me who concentrates on herself. Yet, right now, I simply lack the energy and desire to involve myself in anything.

So tell me—what makes me such a horrible person that people who claim to love me, claim I am important to them, claim I have made a positive difference in their life, claim multitudes of great things, what makes them run off and forget to tell me why. What makes them deny their claims? What is wrong with me?

It wasn't supposed to be that way with XY. I kept my eyes open and was still ripped apart.

I sit here in a quiet state of mind. Reflections of nothing fill me. Suddenly, brain waves begin to vibrate for no reason at all. Agitation. Fear. Craziness. Everything comes upon me at once. So close to the edge and yet so far away. I look over the cliff. It would be an endless fall. There is nowhere to land. That is when I step back. My intelligence overpowers the emotions of my mind. To fall off the cliff looks more terrifying than staying where I am. I turn around. I walk away from the cliff. Everything will be fine until the next cliff appears. Whenever that may be. I don't know. I don't care. Will the drop off the cliff always be more terrifying than the here and now? I don't know.

I am running scared. As fast as I can. I'm running and running. When will this terror stop? Where am I going? I am out of breath. And still I am lost. Dear God, please help me. It is so dark. Screaming at the top of my lungs, I keep going on and on. Does it never end? Does it? I can't help it, God. Why don't you let me stop? Do I have to keep going? My breath. I am losing my breath. Swirls. Swirling. It is all surrounding me. I can't stand it. No, no. Please.

After the second session, Harry asked me to take the MMPI, the Minnesota Multiphasic Personality Inventory. The MMPI is a long yes/no questionnaire used to determine certain facets of one's personality. My results bewildered poor Harry. The results gave him some clues that there was more to my difficulties than met the eye. I was not simply pining for XY. Harry was the first person ever to see that my façade related in no way, shape, or form to the lack of personhood within me. Evidently, the MMPI results gave Harry a few concerned thoughts. Harry sent me to a psychiatrist.

Dr. Jay listened to my babbling for an hour and sent me back to Harry, saying that the problem with me was I hadn't dated in high school. True, the boys hadn't come knocking, but there was more to this depression of mine than a lack of dates. Come on, Dr. Jay, ask questions about more than high school. I have always felt that Dr. Jay had an agendum of answers waiting for me—he asked the questions that led to the answers he had in mind. That one measly hour (and to a psychiatrist an hour is only forty-five minutes) was no help to either Harry or me.

I ended up seeing Harry every week for a couple of years with a couple of diversionary paths here and there. He was a Christian, which was very important to me. He was working on his doctorate in psychology, which appealed to my intellect. Harry often worked through my intellect as his way of getting to my emotional difficulties. Harry assigned books for me to read or gave me other assignments such as goal-setting or analyzing my thoughts and feelings. The most precious part of our counseling sessions came when Harry prayed for me. I needed a lifeline to God, and since I seemed unable to find one, I viewed Harry's prayers as the connection I was missing. Maybe God would listen to Harry. He sure wasn't listening to me. Or was he? Only time, distance and a cleared head would tell.

I had begun seeing Harry in the spring. By fall, I was worse instead of better. I heard a voice repeatedly telling me to kill myself. "Drive off a cliff," it would say. "How fast can you drive into the wall?" I didn't know where these questions were coming from and didn't recognize the thoughts as my own, but I didn't really care.

XY and I shared a birthday month and as fall approached so did the anniversary of our birthday adventure to Boulder Falls. The memories of the previous year worked their way into my thoughts giving my brain a twirl and a swish with a little blender pulsing thrown in to really mix me up.

Thoughts that were not my thoughts began to build with unforeseen intensity. I was surprised each morning. I did not expect to wake up. I certainly did not expect to wake up to nonstop mind torture.

For the first time, my façade cracked and became visible to those around me. Rose, a coworker and friend, was the first. She and I worked closely together on a special project and came to know one another rather well. I could share my XY adventures and tales of woe with Rose. She had a solid foothold on common sense reality and a great sense of humor. I reached out to Rose in a way I had never done before. Days when I was hanging by a spider's thread while walking tiptoe on the high wire, Rose would listen to my pain and fear and grief. Rose was an anchor of reality and compassion.

I am surprised her hearing lasted with all the verbiage I threw her way. Oh, how I droned on and on with my tales of woe regarding XY.

I have always appreciated Rose, but until this moment I don't know that I appreciated her enough. Rose was my first lifesaver. She was, perhaps, more aware of my downward spiraling than I was. There came a day when Rose, my boss, and the school psychologist at the elementary school where I taught held a secret meeting debating what to do with me. The end result was a trip to the psychiatric ward.

Getting up in the morning was no small feat. First, she had to convince herself that she still existed. Next came the prolonged agony of wishing she did not exist. "Why am I still here, God? Didn't you want me, God? How come I have to stay here in this disgusting presence of myself?" Lili would lie there fighting silent tears, not wanting to live and not having the courage to do anything about it. She would eventually roll over and discover that the clock now read 6:45. Fear would seize her heart, and Lili would leap out of bed, dress and be on her way to work in less than fifteen minutes. No shower. No deodorant. Possibly wrinkled clothes. She did brush her teeth. If she thought about it, Lili might run a brush through her hair. Without a mirror, of course.

Work. What an ugly word. Lili loved the children. They were the saving part of the day. If it weren't for the children Lili would probably have the courage to die. But, she couldn't do that to the children. One little boy attached himself tightly to her heart. She was the only person he almost trusted. On this particular day, Lili called her boss and told her that she was coming in to work, but would work only with Sal, the boy attached so to her heart. Lili also told her boss that she could not find her shoes.

When I got to work I sought out Rose, but couldn't find her. I left a cryptic message on her desk about "still being here." When I couldn't find Rose, I went on upstairs and worked with Sal. Sal and I read a book, and then Sal drew a picture to go with the story. We decided to go show Ms. Woods, the principal and my boss. When we got to the office, the secretary told us that Ms. Woods was in a meeting. Sal and I decided to sit and wait. We sat on the bench, swinging our legs, chatting unaware of the secret conference being held on the other side of the door.

What I remember happening next takes on a bit of a surreal quality as if I didn't actually experience it. My next recollection is of Rose and Ms.

Woods driving me to a nearby psychiatric hospital which also happened to be where Harry was a therapist. Harry gave me a choice between two hospitals. One hospital was covered by my insurance and did not include Harry. The other hospital was where Harry was associated, and my insurance would not cover the costs. It was a dilemma. Harry gave me overnight to choose on the condition I was not left alone. Rose, bless her heart forever, volunteered to stay with me. Truly a good friend.

Rose had a family and a life of her own. Her generosity of spirit carried me through some tough times and through normal everyday routines. Rose was a blessing in my life. In staying with me at my apartment that day and night, Rose protected me and her family. I later learned that we didn't stay at her house because if I tried to kill myself she didn't want her young sons to see it. Makes perfect sense to me.

The night before entering the hospital was weird because it was a rather pleasant evening. Rose and I went out for Chinese at an elegant restaurant. We chatted about nothing in particular and laughed at how Ms. Woods had attached herself to the fact that I couldn't find my shoes. Then we went home. When we got to my place, Rose saw for certain that all was not right with me. She later told me that she hadn't realized how far gone I was until she watched me pace that evening. I paced for hours while silly laughter erupted from my throat. It was such an odd space in which to be. I felt as if I were in a bell jar with the air being sucked out and hearing a tinny noise of an unknown source. I also felt a bit on display. Some of my insides were leaking out where others could see. It was eerie. Meanwhile, Rose was my guardian angel, chatting about nothing in particular with silent pauses here and there. She was my safety net.

Rose would spend the night with Lili. It was decided. Lili would not be left alone; she could not be left alone. Lili was glad for the company. Still, driving off a mountain at full speed seemed a plausible comforting idea. With a heart pounding and roaring in her ears, fists clenched more tightly than super glue holds, and a glistening of sweat coating her body, Lili paced. It was a determined pace, purpose unknown; her ability to stop did not exist. Every step brought her closer to the edge of no return, yet kept her from getting there. Lili had to pace. It was her only thread of control, her only containment. Rose sat in her makeshift bed watching. The intense pacing frightened her. Rose attempted light conversation not daring to show her fears. Rose was a good, caring person. Lili would love her always for this gift of true friendship, but for now she could only pace. Thoughts raced through Lili's mind. They came and went with such speed and confusion, Lili could not decipher them. Some of the thoughts did not seem to be her own. She knew they were in her head, but the thoughts seemed separate from herself, as though someone else were talking. It was the suicide thought that was loudest. Thoughts of driving off a mountain were intrusive, invasive, yet Lili could not tell who was thinking this thought. She wanted to be rid of the suicidal thought, yet it enticed her with relief. Driving off the mountain would stop the pain, dispel the anger. Driving off the mountain would end the night of tortured thought. Rose fell asleep, and Lili paced until, in utter exhaustion, she fell onto her bed in restless slumber, thoughts racing confusedly even in her sleep.

The ride to the hospital had Lili feeling like an empty shell might feel when the animal inside dies or moves on. Her body felt a hollowness tingling with anxiety. Relief mingled with wariness of the unknown. She was merely a shell being moved to safety. Rose and Ms. Woods were allowed to walk with Lili to the psychiatric unit. The doors to the floor were locked. No way in or out without someone from inside pushing a buzzer. The hall was long, silent. Every step echoed protection. Lili began to look at the whole event as something new to learn. Her spirits lifted to the relief that could come here on the locked psychiatric ward. A sense of nervous peace began to replace the hollow anxiety. Perhaps being in a safe place would be a good thing.

When we arrived at the hospital, I was taken to an examining room where, of course, I was examined. "Who is the president?" "What day is it?" "How many fingers am I holding up?" "What color is a pink elephant?" Questions to determine if I were crazy or not. I evidently passed the test for I was sent straight up to the psych ward.

Thoughts landed me in the locked psych unit of the local hospital. The thoughts were not my own; that was my opinion. I didn't know who the thoughts belonged to, but I was certain they were not mine. Some people would try to argue me out of such an opinion; others completely ignored my complaint of someone else's thoughts being in my head. I, however, knew I was right and asked the only appropriate question: Whose thoughts were in my head? But no one, it seemed, heard me.

Nine

There is a certain relief and satisfaction upon entering a locked psych unit. Finally, some of the façade can relax. You can admit that all is not right with the world. Being in the psych unit allowed me to relax my defenses against myself. Nothing bad was going to happen.

Once upstairs, I had to bid my caretakers goodbye. It was both a bit of a relief and a bit scary when Ms. Woods and Rose left. Having never been identified as crazy before, I didn't know what to expect. What I didn't expect was Dr. Claws, psychiatrist number two.

Dr. Claws came into the little room. He was short, fat and covered with white hair. Lili was wary. Her last visit with a psychiatrist had been useless. He had blamed everything wrong on a lack of boyfriends in high school. He had listened but hadn't heard.

The first thing Lili noticed about Dr. Claws was his glass of pink stuff. For the months she saw him, Dr. Claws always had a glass of pink stuff in his hand. Lili could never decide if it were a pink squirrel, strawberry milk, or Pepto Bismol.

Lili would develop a strong dislike for Dr. Claws. He, like the other shrink, listened but did not hear. Lili told him about having thoughts in her head that she didn't think were her thoughts. She told him it was as if somebody else were thinking in her head. Dr. Claws waved this information aside, telling her that if it was in her head, she was the one thinking it. He declared her to be histrionic. Dr. Claws, in Lili's opinion, was useless. He was also a liar. Lili was in the hospital for ten days. Dr. Claws met with her four to five times, never for more than fifteen minutes. When Lili received the itemized statement from the hospital, he had charged the hospital for daily forty-five minute sessions. No, Lili did not care for Dr. Claws at all. The jerk.

Dr. Claws looked, sadly enough, a bit like Santa Claus. The big difference between Dr. Claws and Santa was that Dr. Claws was neither jolly nor giving.

I always felt that he was a bit bored with me, with my case. He seemed unable to make a connection with me. Or was it I who could not make a connection with him? I am not sure which came first—my disgust with Dr. Claws himself or that blasted glass of pink stuff always in his hand. Maybe Santa had acid reflux problems.

Anyway, Dr. Claws sat and pretended interest, drank pink stuff, and prescribed medication that did not solve any problems. He was not part of the relief of being locked away.

Some of the relief at being in a safe environment came out in humorous ways. The nurses' station was an island. I walked round and round the nurses' station to relieve pent up tension. One side of this island was a part of the hallway leading out into the free world. Sometimes my pacing led me down this hallway. One day, feeling rather impish, I stopped in that hallway, turned to the nurses' station and said, "Hey, it would be pretty easy to bolt from here!" You never saw people freeze into battle mode any faster. They were perched to go after me! I just laughed and laughed. Boy, it felt good. I felt free for that brief joking moment. The staff, however, put tape across the floor and told me I wasn't allowed to cross it. I just laughed with glee.

There were people on that floor with even less a sense of the world's reality than I, but generally the locked psych unit was filled with ordinary everyday people agonizing in emotional pain. Being in the hospital was my first experience that I was not the only person living with the sense of spiraling downward in pain and despair. At the time, I didn't appreciate the fact that all these people were my peers. We connected with one another with unique magnetism. "Here," we thought, "is someone who understands." The various therapists had words and ideas and perhaps a tinge of insight, but a fellow patient, now that was understanding. What was sad was the policy that we were not allowed to contact one another once out of the hospital. Perhaps they thought we'd become coconspirators in some dark and evil plan.

Group therapy was the worst. Lili felt naked to the world in group. Her normally self-protective walls were bombarded with bayonets poking at her fears and beliefs. She attempted to hide, to become invisible, but it didn't work. Jab, jab, jab. Tell us about today, Lili. What are you feeling? I see you still won't talk Lili. Stop the hiding. Jab, jab, jab. Every time the staff leading the group spoke to Lili, she felt like a spotlight came on over her head. And any time a fellow patient spoke to her, the spotlight shown in her face. Group therapy scared the hell out of Lili. Her entire life had been spent hiding and protecting her privacy. All that was gone with group therapy. Jab, jab, jab. Why do you just sit there? Why don't you talk? They didn't understand. All those years of hiding behind a mask, of appearing to all who knew her as cheerful. She'd even written a poem called *Smiling Faces*. Lili knew the smile was often a cover up for the darkness within. She who smiled with great frequency was filled with rage and fear. People scared her. "What if they find out?" Lili worried over others discovering her secrets. Lili worried over discovering her secrets herself. Once her horridness was discovered, what would come from being discovered? She only knew it would be bad. It might even destroy her. In group therapy, all those people watching, talking and probing were attempting to drag her insides out for all the world to see. Group therapy was unsettling. Group therapy was all one's fears and inadequacies rolled into a huge puss ball then burst by the pressure and drenched in hydrogen peroxide to foam for all the world to see. Group therapy was horrible.

Smiling faces
Smiling faces everywhere
None of them sad
None of them bad
All of them just around.

You're sad on the outside
Cracked on the in.
You wonder what all of these
People are doing.
Them and their grin.

Leering away at you
Smug faces. Smug grins.
Always watching you
Never seeing you
For you are never there.

Smiling faces hang in places
One hardly ever sees
The mask is smiling

The mask must smile
For hate is behind the scene.

Inside is disheveled, broken
Waiting to be repaired
But no one can repair it.
None with the smiling faces

The smiling heart
Is the smile that's real
The mask must drop
so the wound may heal
But where is the heart,
the heart that is real?

There were many types of group activities. Group therapies, group recreation, just lots of groups. We, the patients, were expected to be at every group meeting and to be there on time. However, I often got the impression that these rules didn't apply to the staff. They were late practically every time. We began making up words to Christmas tunes expressing our angst over their lateness. The staff was unappreciative. "On the fifth day of groups we patients got so mad. We flung woven baskets at the staff. Then we sat and glared, brushed our hair, twice we stamped our feet. And refused to participate."

Group therapy could also be interesting. The staff would attempt compassion and understanding. They would try to lead us toward a more "normal" frame of mind. The problem was, some of the staff just didn't get it. And there was much to be "got."

I listened to the man-boy in utter astonishment. He knew nothing about depression. Nothing! The man-boy was standing in front of a group of us inpatients telling us how once we've hit bottom there is nowhere to go but up. I leaped to my feet to express my opinion. "Hey, man-boy! There is no bottom. You feel like you're as far down as you can go, and then the damn steam shovel comes along and digs the hole deeper and darker. There is no tangible bottom. There is no ultimate bottom. No siree, man-boy, that steam shovel just keeps on appearing and digging; to stop it takes strength. You have to find your strength in order to climb your way out. And man-boy, my strength is missing!"

I plopped down into my seat, slumped down and crossed my arms. Then came a burst of applause and cheers. The other inpatients were upholding my words. "Yep, that's right, Lili." "Way to tell 'em, Lili." "There ain't no bottom. That steam shovel's working on me this very minute!" Man-boy just stood there with a perplexed look upon his face. He didn't get it. You could tell by looking at him that he couldn't fathom the unending depths of depression. His eyes asked, "Weren't all these people in the hospital because they'd hit bottom?" I looked at Man-boy and felt sorry for him. He just didn't get it.

Funny, I've been locked in the psych ward twice, and both times I left with pleasant memories. Okay, so I hated the first hospital—but I did enjoy the jokes and songs.

Apparently, I was angry; my entire being and body were filled with rage. But with what was I angry? Was I angry with XY and that whole disaster? Was I angry at me? It was me who was the focus of possible death. The anger blossoming in time-lapse photography style was a surprise to me. Its existence. Its rapid outward growth. Its ferocious intensity. All the hurts in my life balled up into one big malignant growth of anger. I think the core of this era of anger (for there would be more) was the result of disbelief in my own reality. XY told me that my reality was not real. I believed him with horror.

Dear Harry,

Suppose one morning you woke up and your wife wasn't in bed with you. You wouldn't be alarmed, but maybe surprised. You get up and look in the kids' room on your way to the kitchen. They are not in their beds. The house is noisy with silence, but you are busy with thoughts of the coming day. No one is in the kitchen when you get there. In fact, you find yourself to be the only person in the house. There is no note in the usual place. You are surprised, but unconcerned. As you dress for the day, you chuckle over a pile of silly little gifts from your kids and the card from your wife—all a part of your anniversary celebration last night. You wonder where your family is and get ready to leave for the day.

As you leave the house, movement catches your eye. You turn your head and what? It's your wife and children coming out of the house next door. Your wife is driving the kids to school. They smile. You smile. Everybody waves. But, it is as if there is a glass window. The kids don't run to you. They get into the car without another glance. So does your wife. You jokingly yell, "What about a hug?" She looks at you as if you are nuts and drives away.

At the end of the day, you are still alone. Calls home are unanswered. And when you get home, it is just you.

You see your wife next door again. A few verbal exchanges in a pleasant and surprised manner (from your wife) put you into shock. She claims the two of you were never married. That the children are only hers. She completely denies your special evening only the night before.

At home, you search the house. Pictures, mementos, marriage license, birth certificates, their clothing, her makeup and needlepoint. It is all there.

Your wife doesn't deny having loved you. Though she doesn't confirm it either. She doesn't say she left you. She simply says that you were never married.

You have all the proof. But, your wife ignores it and acts as if you are someone she has met casually. And everyone else seems to accept this as natural. They don't say anything. The kids call you Mr. Harry.

The only one who knows the truth, or voices the truth, is you. You have the proof in your mind, your heart and your paraphernalia.

How do you feel?

How long before you will accept that which feels false?

Your wife didn't just leave you. She claims you were never even married.

To throw away the marriage license and the clothes and the needlepoint is throwing away the only proof you have that you're right. The wedding ring—do you take it off?

What can you do with your craziness that isn't craziness but is treated as such?

What can you do with your love that is neither accepted nor pushed away? What can you do with your anger? Your wife will not respond because she denies there was a marriage, so what can there be to be angry about? Now, you can't deal with your anger with her. You can't deal with the anger in yourself because you are too busy feeling crazy.

Time goes on, and you become generally used to the situation but do you accept it? Do you *ever* accept that there was no marriage?

What do you feel? What do you think? What do you do?

And every time you get a little more used to this craziness, your wife makes a slip in wording, voice or look or you bump into some "artifact" you didn't get packed away when getting rid of visual reminders. How long would all this last? How would you deal with it?

What does a person do in such circumstances? I became angry. Angry at the uncertainty of my reality. Angry at the engulfing, growing confusion. This was the beginning of a more conscious awareness of my various realities. I was starting to see more clearly how other people had a different sense of reality than I did.

Intertwined with this blossoming of anger and reality crisis was my constant, continuous craving to be known completely and loved no matter what.

Harry, tonight I want to scream at you. I feel like a child. I want you to make it all better. And you won't. I want you to take away my fear and pain and anger and panic. I want you to make me well. I just want it to happen and slip into place. I want it all to go away and not come back.

And I am afraid. I am afraid that the next round of pain will hurt even more. I am so filled with pain that any more must be unbearable. It is as if I am already screaming so hard that if I have to scream any louder or longer or harder, I will turn inside out and scream myself into oblivion.

The more I think about it, the more uncertain I am about this anger thing. I don't know. What am I angry about? With whom am I angry? Am I angry with myself? For loving. For wanting. For not being whatever it is I am not? For not knowing what it is that is wrong with me, for wanting to be loved and knowing it will never happen.

I hate this. I really hate this. Why can't I just be?

I question: How can I hurt any more? How can I feel more pain? And I know that I can. But, how much more can I take and survive?

The hospital stay included a week or two of day-treatment with more delightful group therapy. Nothing much happened here other than my birthday. I longed to tell the group it was my birthday. I wanted them to bring joy to this day for me. I wanted them to know without my having to tell them. I wanted, I wanted, I wanted.

After the group session was over and everyone had left, I burst into tears. I was a nothing after all.

As I was leaving the room, the counselor and a manic patient were out in the hallway. "Why are you crying?" they demanded. "Why didn't you tell us?" I cried even more. How could I tell them it was the anniversary of the most wonderful birthday of my adult life and an anniversary of wanting to hold hands with someone who did not want to be touched by me? It was an awesome birthday filled with bittersweet bitterness. Oh, how I wanted to be loved. XY, why couldn't you love me?

All my life I have wanted just one person to accept me completely as I am. If unconditional love is the first requirement, then we may as well forget it. Why do people keep lying to me? I love you. Goodbye forever. I love you. Here is the list of everything wrong with you. I love you. Now go away.

This need, this craving, for love was what it was all about. What I would later come to realize was that love of self must come first. At this point, however, I was a long way from loving myself. I was a long way from knowing who my self was.

After almost three weeks of hospital care I was deemed safe enough to return home. It felt good to be in my own little nest safe from the world and myself. This turned out to be a mere pause in my journey down that spiraling road of darkness, but at the time I only knew it felt good to be home.

Ten

For a year or so things moved along in deterioration mode. Then one day, pictures began flashing through my head. The dark man came and got me. He made me suck on his peepee stick. He bounced me up and down on himself. The pictures raced through my head. Flashing bright stills and movies whirled by. I couldn't get them out of my head. The pictures bombarded me, never ending. Finally, I started drawing the pictures flashing through my head. It was the only way I could calm them down. I ran around to various people (i.e. Harry and Rose) asking, "Is this what it looks like?" "Can it happen this way?"

I was frantic with fear. Who could have done this to me? Was I still a virgin? Why wouldn't the pictures stop? Why, why, why? Panic and frenzy filled the spaces in my brain. The pictures clenched my heart with fear.

These nonstop pictures had me questioning in my mind every male I had ever known. With these pictures, movies actually, bombarding my inner eyes with unrelenting never-ending flashes came panic, more anger, frustration, and yes, folks, more pain. I wanted to see man-boy and shout at him that I was right. "See! I told you, man-boy. There is no bottom. Things can get worse! What? You can't see me? Well, gee, could it be that my hole's bottom is further than you can see? Huh, man-boy?" Oh, how I wanted to shout at him.

The abuse felt very real. The movies playing in my mind were interactive with my senses. Yes, it was horror becoming more horrific daily.

Frequently, I would become scared for no known reason. I would be in the middle of reading or watching television when boom! this scared feeling would come. My face would tighten, and I would start darting furtive looks around the room. Was he here? Was I in danger? I would then go to bed and sit curled up with my pillow clenched in front of me as a form of defense.

Needless to say, I hadn't reached the bottom of my personal dark pit.

The night lurked before her endless with despair. Lili lay on her bed, the rolling wheel cutter blade sparkling in the light. In a trance, she rolled the blade gently back and forth. How hard could she push before the blood would come? Back and forth. Add a little pressure. Back and forth. Push a little harder. Back and forth. The lure of injury and death was a bit intoxicating. Life was a blur. The rotary cutter glistened hypnotically in the lamplight. Lili stared at it. The blade began to have a life of its own. Slowly, slowly, the rotary cutter continued across her arms, her wrists. Lightly, gently, it glided. Not yet cutting, but wanting to. The blade wanted to slice away at Lili. Something told Lili she had better talk to somebody so she dialed the crisis hot line number. The woman answering the phone had a pleasant voice. She and Lili talked back and forth. Lili needed to talk. She thought talking to someone would break the rotary cutter's power. She couldn't tell if it was working. The blade just kept moving.

I don't know what was going on that night. Of course, I often did not know what was going on. I remember feeling as if I were in a trance. I remember sitting there rolling the blade across my arms, over my wrists. Light glinted off the blade. Back and forth, back and forth. My mind wandered into a wondering state. Wondering what it would feel like to cut myself. What if I slashed my face (a frequent thought)? What would happen? Would anyone care? The thoughts were not pleasant thoughts, yet they seemed perfectly sane and calm and natural to me.

I called the suicide hot line. I figured if I talked to someone, maybe the trance would go away. I just needed to talk to someone. The hot line lady had a real sweet voice. She seemed rather nice. She spoke softly, gently, soothingly. What I didn't know was that the hot line lady was on a mission. We chatted about the fact that I was rolling a rotary cutter across my arms—not with too much pressure, but with the desire to hurt myself. This sweet little hot line lady talked about how people would miss me, about how much there was to live for. She was so sweet, so kind, so gentle. And she was new at her job, or so she said. This sweet little hot line lady asked if she could put me on hold while she answered another line. She said she was new and wasn't sure how to run the phones. Naïve little me, I said sure I would wait. In a short time, the sweet little hot line lady was back on the phone with me asking questions, talking to me about how important I was. Then the doorbell rang.

It was after nine o'clock in the evening. I don't answer my door after nine at night unless I know who it is. I told the sweet little hot line lady that my doorbell was ringing, but I wasn't going to answer it. She encouraged me to answer the door and said she would wait until I got back. So I said, sure, why not. I put the phone down and went to the door. Hmmm, I thought, there is an ambulance outside. I wonder who is sick. I opened the door, and there stood six policemen and two paramedics. As soon as I opened the door, they walked right in. The policemen searched the house with flashlights. The paramedics chased me to my bedroom. I picked up the phone and hung up on that bitch lady who had lied to me. I leaped upon my bed screaming. I grabbed the phone and called Harry. There was no answer. I left a message and hung up. The paramedics were talking their trash trying to get me to go with them. I was standing on my bed screaming at the top of my lungs. Then the phone rang. I dived for it before the paramedics could get it. It was Harry. He just happened to be at the office when my message came in. He asked me what was going on. I cried that the police were searching my house and that the paramedics were trying to grab me. He asked to speak with the paramedic. I gave her the phone. She spoke a few words with Harry and gave the phone back to me. Harry told me to go with the paramedics, so I did. He also promised to meet me at the hospital.

The policemen asked me for the rotary cutter. They took it away from me. I never saw it again. The hospital claimed they never saw it. The police department claimed they never had it. One of those policemen stole my rotary cutter. I went with the blonde lady paramedic to the ambulance. She checked me over and talked a lot. At least, I wished she would quit talking. Being in the back of the ambulance, I had no idea where we were going. But then I remembered that the paramedic had told Harry where we were headed. The paramedic kept poking and prodding and questioning. She took my blood pressure twice. I tried to ignore her while trying to guess our route and where we were at on that route. We finally arrived at the hospital.

Lili felt a bit airy, as if she weren't there while the paramedics walked her through the emergency room. Nothing was real. The bright white light became the sun on a summer's afternoon. Lili wondered if she might get a tan. Skin cancer wouldn't be so bad. Someone called her name. Lili blinked into awareness. Clean cut edges of reality stared Lili in the face. Walls, counters, corners. Straight smooth lines. They fascinated the mind of Lili. After a seemingly endless journey, Lili was placed in a partitioned off area containing a bed. Her blood pressure was taken for a third time. Then she was left alone. Lili could hear the murmuring activity of the ER. She could not understand any voices until she heard the distinctive voice of her savior.

I was escorted into the emergency room and put behind a curtain far away from the other ER patients. I sat there for quite awhile before anyone came to talk to me. Then I heard the voice of freedom. Harry was there! My savior! I heard him talk to the doctor. He told the doctor that I had never actually hurt myself, merely made the motions. Then he came to talk to me and find out what was going on. After what seemed like hours, I was released. The problem was I had to find a cab that would accept a check as payment. Thankfully, I found one. Or should I say a nurse found one. I wasn't allowed to use the phone. On the ride home, I made a promise to myself that I would never call the suicide hot line again. That sweet little hot line lady was a liar, a sweet talker. She made me mad. (She did her job.[2])

For days, maybe even months, I planned my escape route from the police and paramedics for the next time they knocked on my door. I would wear all black. I would escape out the back door and hide behind the shed. I would be as invisible as a cat burglar and sleuth my way around spying on the police and paramedics as they searched for me in vain. They would never find me, and I would rejoice with glee. But, I never had to call the suicide hot line again. Hallelujah!

Thoughts of the possible sexual abuse continued to plague me. I feared the memories were mere fabrication of my confused mind. I also feared the memories came from actual events of my life that I had blocked out.

Something weird just happened, and, in a way, is still going on. It is as if I am in two realities. I will describe the way I am sitting and then write what happened. Look how tiny I'm writing, as if it is a secret. I keep looking up to make sure nobody is there. Every few seconds my eyes glance up. Once in awhile I look all around to make sure he isn't here. It is as if I am play-acting, but it is very real. I always sit cross-legged when I write sitting up in bed. Tonight I have a pillow stuffed between my legs for safety. On the one side of reality, I know I am an adult and alone in my bed. The other reality is I am little and scared and waiting. I am not going to let him inside of me. Over the pillow I have my blankets and on top of that another pillow then the writing

---

2   AND I MUST ADD THIS DECLARATION: PLEASE CALL THE SUICIDE HOTLINE OR 911 IF YOU ARE IN AN EMERGENCY SITUATION. THIS IS WRITTEN AS I EXPERIENCED IT IN MY EMOTIONAL STATE OF THE MOMENT, NOT AS I VIEW IT IN THIS MORE NORMAL STATE OF MIND. WHO KNOWS WHAT HORROR MAY HAVE HAPPENED HAD I NOT CALLED THE HOTLINE.

board. I am all hunched up. My face feels stubbornly and tightly set. I think my mind is beginning to come back to having one reality, one present reality. I just managed to take a deep breath and relax a little bit. Now for what happened:

I am not sure how it began. I know I was arguing with myself about who the man could be before it started, but I don't remember if there was any space between the two. I was lying down, and "suddenly" my legs were wide apart and the man was inside of me. I could feel this big lump inside of me. My legs got further apart, and I felt it more. It didn't hurt. It was as though I were used to the feeling. It was as if I suddenly woke up even though I wasn't asleep. I began crying, "Please don't go inside of me. Please don't go inside any more." Then he was out, and I slammed my legs together and went nuts screaming, "Don't you touch me anymore." "I'm not letting you go inside me anymore." I cried and cried and kept repeating myself and squeezing my legs together as tight as possible. A couple of times my muscles would relax and my legs would separate. I would scream and squeeze them back together as tightly as possible. I ended up whimpering, crying and pleading all curled up in a ball at the head of my bed. And then the "two realities" set in. A very small young frightened me and an adult living as a baby but working at getting back into the present. I am not there yet. I am very tight. I do not have a split personality, but two mes are definitely here. Should I be saying mind meet emotion? Emotion meet Mind … This would be the second time they were both present in awareness at the same time. I am afraid to let my legs out. He will come in me again. I know he will. I can feel him now. Go away feeling. Go away big bad man. Stay away and don't come back. Two of me are here.

Fabricated memories. It bothers me. It has bothered me all along. Being as objective as possible I can see both sides. Sad to say, it seems to me more points to the abuse being real rather than fabricated. The strongest part of me does not want to believe that sexual abuse occurred. I have done my best to prove it didn't occur. But, what I come up with is very little. 1) Who would do this? I have no memory of anyone. 2) No apparent physical "symptoms" when I was a kid. At least none ever mentioned. That is it. I find nothing else to prove the "memories" false.

Evidence for its being truth is much easier. Too easy. It brings tears to my eyes. It makes me sad.

THE EVIDENCE POINTING TOWARD SEXUAL ABUSE:

- Always feeling different, set apart (at least since age ten)
- Fear of being around people
- Fear of dark-haired hairy men
- Terror of the pictures flashing through my head
- Lifelong fear of people finding out about me; not knowing what it was I was afraid they would find out
- Recognition of myself in what I have now read concerning sexual abuse
- Feeling that I am crazy
- Extreme dichotomy of intellect and emotion
- Neediness for closeness yet always running away
- Withdrawal behaviors
- Turning anger on myself or holding it in to the point of not recognizing its existence
- Needing honesty yet terrified of truth
- Inability to make and keep rules or boundaries for myself in regard to others
- Extreme need for love and never feeling loved
- The drawings
- Body memories—a phenomenon unheard of until I began experiencing them
- Power given to objects over me and my mind
- Increased need to feel safe
- Intense anger when it comes and literally not knowing where it comes from or what to do with it

THINGS POSSIBLY LEADING TO "FABRICATION":

- Harry's two questions regarding trauma and sexual abuse asked after my childlike frantic bawling session in the waiting area
- Mother's wondering about me being molested and not telling her
- My own dramatization and perseveration on things known and desired
- My wanting an explanation for my life—something to prove I am not crazy or a split personality
- My lack of known physical symptoms

I found it much easier to find arguments against a fabrication of memory rather than for fabrication. Looking at each point individually, I would not have thought of sexual abuse. Looking at the list as a whole, it seemed that major trauma of some sort most likely had occurred. Something more than temper flair-ups.

When I viewed the five possible fabrication explanations, I could not find them strong enough to discount the possibility of recovered memory. Also, there was no purpose for the fabrication. I gained nothing. I would not gain love, relationship, or anything else. Therefore, for me at this point, fabrication made no sense. Why would I make such a thing up?

Then again, I would think, there might be an emotional advantage to fabrication of memory—there might also be an advantage if it were all real memory. It would be an explanation for my emotional denial, a reason not to claim "ugly" emotions as my own.

In some respects, the question of fabrication was not important. As long as there was no false memory of who the perpetrator was, the only thing of true consequence would be what came from it in the end. Something good must be its end. That was my decision.

During this time of questioning, my constant, nonstop, ongoing prayer had been for only truth to enter my brain. I did not believe that God would allow me to have false memories.

The issue of sexual abuse would continue to haunt me for a very long time, years in fact. Would I ever find answers? Would I ever know for sure?

Eleven

The two and one half years with Harry were turbulent and filled with more downward spirals of turmoil than upward movement toward emotional health and well-being. As time went by, crises seemed to come one right after another.

Thoughts of self-destruction increased. I would start hitting myself or banging my body against the wall. I never felt safe.

To decide that hurting myself is not an option. I can't do that. I don't see any other options. Why do you think I stay in bed? Yelling, hitting a pillow, praying, etc. do nothing more than get me more worked up. So does writing much of the time.

How do I prepare myself for the raging anger I am supposedly going to feel when memory clears and when the perpetrator becomes known? How will I know I am feeling it? I know out of control. I met anger once.

I want to go to a hospital so much. I want a haven for a while to scream and yell and cry and withdraw and act however I want to for a while. But, I don't want all those people. I would be talked at. Or ignored. I just want the safeness. I want my room overlooking the emergency room and parking lot so I can watch the world. I want the screens that are secretly steel bars so no one can get in (and they think it's to keep us from jumping).

I want to chop myself up. Slash, slash, cut, slice, gouge. Destroyed forever so people will stay away from me. I want to be a baby again. I want to start over. I want to kill him. Then I will just be gone.

Last night I had to fight against the urge to slam myself against the wall. This is the first time I have ever wanted to pound and slam at a conscious level. Usually, it is after I slam myself or hit myself that I know about it. I lay for a time pounding and slamming myself in my head. Then I stood on the bed and hit my head against the window a bit. I see the difference in this and other episodes as having a reason other than to feel pain. It was just an energy wanting displacement, and I do not know what that energy represented. I was so bound up I couldn't get to sleep for hours. You are probably thinking, "Good. She didn't hurt herself. We're making progress." That would not be a true statement. I did it inside my head and felt frustration and rising anxiety. Emotionally, it was the same as my not-thought-out-spontaneous self-abuse. Oh, forget it. I can't write what I am trying to say. The desire to hurt myself remains strong, very strong.

I have decided to slice my breasts off. Then people can't notice them and make comments. I wouldn't have a shelf anymore. And while I am at it, I should sew myself up so no one can get in. I don't know what to do with my mouth and tongue and throat. My hands. I can scrape all the skin off. I want to get rid of it all. I am angry, I think. But it is subtle. Very subtle. I mean, I don't feel it. I talk it.

And tonight as I walked down the hall toward my bedroom I started to cry. My safety zone, my place where no cutting or killing will occur, my refuge, my work place, my thinking and remembering place has also become my prison of loneliness. There is no place else to be when I am alone. And there's no place to be with people. My solace and my prison are one and the same, and that is some word with more scope and depth than sad. I just don't know what the word is.

Through all of this, I managed to work and pay bills. Between hanging onto the fact of God's ever steady presence and that inherited stubborn streak, I managed to plow through daily life. Life was an effort, and somehow I kept on.

Harry and psychiatrist number three, Dr. Forest (who was an improvement over the others), told me I was doing all right. This was so frustrating! I felt as if nobody were hearing me. I knew I wasn't all right. My steam shovel was digging the hole deeper and faster than I could grab hold and climb up. I just kept spiraling downward. That was my experiential perception.

You say I am doing all right. You are wrong. I am not all right. Okay, so I generally make it through work, force myself to stay in places where I don't feel comfortable, almost eat each day and other stuff deemed "healthy," but I am not okay.

What do I think of myself? I think I was a very stupid child. I think

I want to die and would kill myself if I had any guts. I think there are two of me. I think relationships with people would be different if the stuff hadn't happened. I think I could easily let go of the reality of the present and become lost and immersed in the realities of the past. I think I am ugly and not worth anybody's attention. I think my bedroom is the only safe place outside of counseling and also the most horrid painful place to be. I think what I did was ugly and disgusting.

The one emotion I know for certain that I recognize is fear. I think sadness is becoming more clear. I mean I cry now and know why I am crying. And panic. I recognize panic. I think panic and fear are the emotions to have ruined every relationship I have ever had. They have even had their place with you now and again. Panic once in awhile. Fear fairly steadily. And safeness. You, Harry, are safe. Fear of being thrown to the wolves brings on panic. So I hold on to every safe minute. I am not attached to you the person. It is your representation of safeness. Even the walls are safe. I want a table to fit over my bed.

I saw Dr. Forest today. Psychiatrists. I was there less than 30 minutes. He thinks I am doing fine and do not require more intensive treatment. (It doesn't matter that I only looked at him once, read the enclosed stuff to him, hung on to my coat for dear life and shook the entire time.) Dr. Forest's comments: i) get a cat; ii) continue meds; iii) continue seeing Harry; iv) call again after April 15. (Evidently, taxes are more important than I.)

Telling him of my suicidal and "injuricidal" and hospitalization wishes didn't phase the man. I left in tears. I was almost hoping he'd recommend more intensive therapy. But no, Dr. Forest thinks I am doing fine.

MOOD: At the moment very angry. I don't know at what. I am only just beginning to recognize the mood of anger. Otherwise I don't know.

AT WORK: Usually okay with adults. They don't scare me much. Generally, my temper is in the wings waiting to come out. By afternoon, I am usually agitated and anxious wanting to get out of there. I have to work extremely hard to contain myself. I am a great actor. With students, I manage. I maintain. I contain.

SOCIALLY: I attend more things with more regularity. It is an effort with the exception of women's Bible Study. Whenever XY is also in attendance I struggle, but twice now have managed to enjoy myself. I fall apart once I get home.

AT HOME: My most horrible place to be because this is where my shell of protection is not always in place. I will suddenly begin screaming or pounding the walls with my fists, arms, or head. I might kick or throw things. These behaviors seem to come without warning. They simply explode out of me. There are other times when visual contact with an object, generally sharp, brings about a fascination. I stare, play with, or lightly experiment on my arms with it. Other times I withdraw completely to my bed. I do this when I need to feel safe or when I am overwhelmed and need to get away from it all. At the same time I do manage to clean once in a while.

SLEEPING: Back and forth. Sometimes regular. Other times, I am more tired when I wake up than when I went to bed. And then, there are the days I fight to get to sleep or fight to wake up. It is always a surprise.

EATING: I eat maybe two meals a week. The rest of the time it might be a piece of toast or milk or juice or a handful of cereal. I am seldom hungry.

SPIRITUAL: I am angry at God. I fight Him constantly. I don't let him near. I try, but I frequently end up in tears at church. Sometimes I have to leave because I can't handle it.

I am liked. I never said I wasn't liked. Everybody likes me. My stupid list of virtues is a mile long. Being liked and being wanted are *not* the same thing. People like my laughter, my humor, my smiles, my creativity. They like lots of things. But it's all surface crap.

Thus is the present.

My internal pain grew and changed. It began as the mushy core of a pimple and evolved into stubborn solid granite. The pain became so solid I had to admit to its existence. The granite was so fused to me that I had to work to find it and recognize it. The pain was somehow so well protected that I lived with the extremes of being consumed by pain yet felt none of it.

The pain was solid yet was without perimeter. There was no beginning, no end to the pain. It was a cosmos made up of granite waiting to explode.

My pain was composed of all the hurts I had ever experienced. It contained all the "buts" of what people had labeled love. The cracks, filled with fear, were of each and every hurt ever bestowed upon me.

I was in pain.

I wanted to feel. I wanted something other than pain and anger to fill me. I wanted someone to hold my hand. I wanted to be hugged and to feel loved. I wanted to stop hurting so that it would not be an effort to take a bath or wash my hair. I wanted everything horrible to become simply knowledge of events rather than movies flashing through my head. I wanted someone to invent paper that you didn't have to turn over because I was too tired for such a menial task. I wanted. I wanted. I wanted to feel comfortable in my own house outside of my bed.

I was filled with an unending unknown list of things I needed to talk about. Though the need was mine, I couldn't read the list. I couldn't find the list inside of me. All I knew was that there was a cacophony of issues hiding from me in my brain.

As time passed I felt crazier and less attached to the world's reality.

It was really quite depressing. Perhaps that was why Harry determined I was clinically depressed. He knew there was more to it than that, but it was a place to start.

I don't understand how I can be okay and practically suicidal at the same time. And I am. I am feeling crazy, out of control, insane, and suicidal. I am handling work and the students. I want to scream until there is no screaming left in me. I want the bloody suicidal thoughts to go away before they take over and it is too late. I keep asking God to fill my every crack and crevice with Himself. And then, I scream into my pillow because He doesn't seem to answer my plea. Is it because He hasn't filled me or because I don't believe He has or will? Harry, this is so horrible. Please, help me. I am falling apart piece by piece. I can feel each and every piece as it falls. Piece by piece.

It is weird. I can sit and watch myself clean and scrub and do all sorts of good things to my house. Yet, when I look again, nothing has been changed. There is still everything to do. I envision; I don't do. Then I scream at nothing. I will yell at the television or explode yelling at myself or scream at objects or a room.

I can relate to Lizzy Borden. Or I am Dibs[3]? How can I be both Lizzy Borden and Dibs? But I am. They were similar. They both were filled with anger and pain. They both played out their anger and pain. Lizzy used an axe; Dibs used toys and a sandbox.

I spent hours crying in Harry's office and waiting room. Harry told me that I appeared to be a needy child. As that needy child, I wanted Harry to take care of me. I wanted God to fill me with His love.

3   Axline, Virginia M. (1964). Dibs: In Search of Self. NY, New York: Ballantine Books. (This is the story of an emotionally disturbed boy who takes part in play therapy.)

I wanted to scream it all out of me, but it just wouldn't go away. Sigh.

As days and months went by I began to feel even crazier with all that was going on within me. The moving, talking pictures of abuse never left me. I became fearful and agitated. I would sit curled up in a ball in Harry's office not always able to focus on things or be a part of my own therapy. Slowly I slid further down that path of feeling crazy. What was real? What was not-real? Whose memories were right? Was I always wrong in what I remembered? There were no answers. It seemed that there was no way out of this pit of crazy mixed-up depression. I had thoughts at times that I did not recognize as mine, but I didn't know what to do with them. Though Harry listened, I wasn't certain he heard me. I wanted him to hear inside of me. I was only capable of sharing and exposing so much of me. My wish for Harry to see inside of me was so I wouldn't have to figure out how to tell him all that was there. Sometimes I would sit there praying he would just know. Being was a struggle. Being me was even more of a struggle.

Safety these days came in only two places: my bedroom and Harry's office. Harry, the fiend, wouldn't allow me to camp out or live at his office. "Why not?" my head begged. But, no, I was told to go home when my time was up. Being sent home probably had to do more with my crying spells in the waiting room than with my appointment being over. One memorable crying spell stands out.

I don't remember the counseling session. I do remember being in the waiting room crying and sobbing for what seemed to be hours and hours of unrelenting tears. I don't know that more tears have ever been shed by anyone in a single sitting. It felt as if somebody else were crying, and I could hear it happening. Harry kept coming into the waiting room telling me I had to leave. I could hear his voice, but was unable to respond. The sobs were big, deep, buckets-of-water sobs. The tears wouldn't stop. I had no control over them. Logic would say they were my tears. They just didn't feel like mine. It was as if I were sitting in a dark room watching someone under a bright light crying her heart out. She was the focus of my attention with nary an idea that such was the case. All that existed for her were the tears and the pain and the fears. More pain could not have been endured. More fear could not have been clinging to her soul. More tears could not have flowed down swollen cheeks. All of this gut-wrenching clinging emotion came from behind a dam greater in size and strength than any built in history. The tears were essentially the culmination of all that had come before and the gathering of all that was to come.

After the tears of this moment, things began to happen within me that gave me great anxiety. I felt crazier than ever and found it increasingly difficult to focus or stay in the present. Terror of being found out or finding out myself haunted me. I was dancing around the world and its people. I was always searching for answers to questions never asked or found. It wasn't easy.

Being crazy wasn't easy.

Twelve

"This picture feels more real than anything. All the bad things trying to get out at once. Everything is making noise and moving all over the place. Swirling, flying, banging on the bars. Nothing makes sense."

In the year of my craziness, I discovered I was not crazy. The summer had been a mess in my head. My head was filled with noises and pictures. The noise was constant and loud and sounded like a cacophony of monkey screeching. It was unrelenting. I had to work at being aware of real-life interactions. The problem was, I couldn't always see the real world. Pictures flashed through my mind like a strobe-lit slide show. Red. White. Black. Person. Bars. Parachute. Stripes. Mean things. Evil. Bad. Scared.

Hiding. The pictures intensified by the second or so it seemed. Relentless noise. Relentless pictures. In real-life, it only appeared that I was okay. The noise and pictures resulted in my knowing without a doubt that I was crazy. What could be crazier than walking around in the real world without seeing or hearing it? It was bad. And once again, no one knew. My, I was talented. God does give us amazing gifts.

Sometimes the noise seemed to be words that I couldn't understand. "Words, words, words, I'm so sick of words. I get words all day through first from him now from you, is that all you blithers can do?" (from "My Fair Lady") The days were endless. The noise in my head was constant and never-ending. For a long while, the noise made no sense. It was just a mish mash of sound, possibly voices and electricity gone astray. Sometimes I felt that there were people talking in my head, but I could not understand them. The inside of my head held mass confusion. The pictures flashed through my head as the noise escalated and remained never-ending. Swirling colors of black, red, and white. Coming and going. Twirling like a whirling dervish. Constant noise. Constant motion.

One day I decided to walk to the library. It was hot out, nearing 100°, and my house wasn't air conditioned. (So I walked a mile through the heat? Maybe I *was* crazy!) The noise and pictures flashing through my head were growing in volume and intensity. I had to walk slowly in order to walk straight. The noise pummeled at my brain. Pictures blocked comprehension of the visual world surrounding me. Noise. Pictures. More Noise. More Pictures. I couldn't take it anymore.

On this day an eerie yet calming awareness slowly came to my attention. One of the many pieces of noise spoke a little louder than the rest. "Hello," it said.

"Hello," I answered back.

An audible pause in the noise filled the air. Then the voice, a toddler's voice, answered back. "Hi," it said. It was a girl's voice. With this response, the red and white swirls showed themselves to be a settling parachute. In front of the parachute was a little girl.

"Hello, again. Who are you?"

"Vicki." And with that one official contact with the noise in my head, things calmed down for the worse. The red and white parachute came down. The strobe light stopped flashing. Strangely, for the first time in months, there was a certain calmness in my head and in my being. It did not seem strange that Vicki was speaking to me. It did not seem strange that I could talk back to her.

Vicki was definitely a young child. I asked her how old she was. "Two-four" she would state very authoritatively. In the years that followed that was always her answer. "I'm two-four." I asked Vicki why she called to me. She told me that Val would not stop crying.

"Who is Val?" I asked.

"She's little. She won't stop crying."

That very first day of calm but crazy shall remain a picture in my head forever. I can see the bright beautiful blue sky; I hear the trees whispering a soft jingling symphony. The day was glorious, and I heard voices that weren't mine. All in all, a very good day.

Although I was very calm about the conversation with Vicki, I was also terrified. Who was this person in my head? What were all these other noises I heard? These questions brought more questions, and I was filled with angst. It was horrible and wonderful. And interestingly enough, I no longer felt crazy. I don't know how to describe it. Somehow, all that noise turning out to be people in my head talking to me seemed much more sane than all that noise had been. I guess it is all relative. For the next several weeks, I was on the phone constantly with Harry. Plainly speaking, I was freaking out. I know, I know. This sounds as if I am contradicting myself. Yet, I felt all of this at the same time. Weird, isn't it?

This whole experience may sound strange to the millions of truly never-felt-insane sane people out there, but the fact that there was a little girl inside of me who very clearly spoke to me really was beautifully calming.

Vicki told me that the dark man was scaring Val. Val only cried. She couldn't talk. Vicki's job was to protect her and take care of her. But, Vicki couldn't take the crying anymore. She couldn't help Val anymore so she called to me. As if I could do anything about it.

After Vicki, other voices and people became more distinct in my head. It seemed quite reasonable to me that several different people shared my head. Anything was better than the constant static of noise that had plagued me for so long.

I soon discovered I could see the people inside me. Vicki was a little trouper with a sturdy body and a foot she liked to stamp. Val was always against a wall curled up in a ball with a blanket pulled over her head. The Gray and White One was a shadowy arm. I never saw the rest of that person. There were others on occasion. Each with their own things to say, each with their own look.

The discovery of all these people inside me, might have calmed me down inside, but it wrecked havoc with my life.

Let's check the data:

1. I no longer existed, i.e., I had no self.
2. I'd been hospitalized for suicidal ideation.
3. I spent my days crying.
4. I'd been drinking from a baby bottle.
5. I had people who were not me living inside me.

Could it get any worse? Yes, it could.

Thirteen

I am a Prisoner
that I am
I am a prisoner
I'm more than one

I am a prisoner of life
wanting death sometimes more

I am a prisoner of loneliness
held in by my fears

I am a prisoner of intellect
whose emotions don't show

I am a prisoner of anger
too contained and then POW!

I am a prisoner of my past
A past I don't even know

I'm a prisoner of sex
Oral sex. Face unknown.

I'm a prisoner of memories
and a body that knows

I am a prisoner of tears
Of tears aching to flow

I'm a prisoner of a man
Tickling. Giggling. Fingers. Rape.

I am a prisoner of prayer
With a troubled searching soul

I am a prisoner
With no place to go

I am a prisoner.
Held tight. Not let go.

Body memories were the worst. I could taste and feel everything that happened over and over. A penis in my mouth gagging me with its salt. Fingers stroking, tickling. Fingers inside of me jamming and pushing themselves with increasing force. Val would cry. Vicki would get mad. I would experience the sensations. Oh, those terrifying experiences. It was always dark when the man came. I could never see him. Just his shape, a man's shape. I would be in bed, in my car, at work, anywhere, when suddenly my mouth would fill with memories. My body would respond.

"What in bloody hell are you doing?" My little body wanted to scream, "I don't want things in all my holes. You bastard! How dare you trick me into liking that ugly stuff you do! How dare you!" The anger, the rage, the fear were all so real. I could see it, smell it, touch it, taste it with all my senses yet I had no memory of any such things happening to me. It's in my head for some reason. Did it really happen? Did I make it up? It tormented me not to know. At times, I thought I remembered. Then would come the doubts and the lack of memory. What is real? What is not-real? I didn't know. Always I was filled with questions.

It was horrible. I could feel and see and taste and hear it all. Over and over and over. When I went to bed at night, I would smell my underwear trying to discover if I were an adult or little girl that day. Since I did not have a me, my underwear was my daily clue. Usually, they smelled of a little girl's urine. Would I ever be an adult? I didn't know the answer and was afraid of being an adult.

She could feel it coming. The man was coming. The dark man was going to come at any minute. She huddled in her bed waiting. Waiting.

Her body began to twitch and feel things. It was so bad, yet it felt kind of good. She could taste the gook from his peepee stick. Lick it, lick it he would say. Suck it, suck it he would say. He would touch her insides with his fingers, with his mouth. Her body would pulse with fear, with sexual fear that sometimes felt good. It was nonstop. She hated the man. She wanted him to stop coming. She took to sleeping on the bathroom floor with the door closed so he couldn't find her.

Vicki was the one who remembered and fought. Val was the one who experienced it all.

With the realization that many people lived inside me, I wanted to be back in the hospital. There was just too much going on inside of me. The people talked and talked. Vicki yelled a lot. Val cried. Jenny pretended to be a prairie girl. Beth soothed everyone. Some people wanted to end it all. It was confusing, mind boggling. I felt on the edge of reality wanting all that wasn't. I wanted to feel that safe relief again. I wanted to be surrounded by people who truly understood pain and hurt and suicidal thoughts. I did not need to be made safe from myself. I wanted to be safe from the world and all those people inside me. I was hurting so much. I felt lost and alone, yet surrounded by too many people. I wanted the hospital.

How do I want to feel when all by myself? I want to feel comfortable with myself and not be begging for approval. I want to feel emotions without feeling guilty or wrong for feeling them. I want to feel strong so that being uncomfortable in a situation won't set me off in a tailspin. I want to feel capable of standing up for myself and what I know to be true. I want to feel emotions at a "normal" level and recognize what they are. I want to feel strength to pull through this horror within myself rather than rely on others for that strength. I want to feel good to be me. I want....

Throughout the weeks of this summer, I bombarded Harry with phone calls begging for extra sessions. I felt completely out-of-control, like the world was spiraling around me. After a couple months, Harry and I reached a consensus that perhaps another hospital stay might be helpful. Harry had a friend who worked as psychiatrist in a psychiatric unit across the state, "But," said Harry, "you must have goals."

I got agitated. I slammed myself around on my bed. I went to the living room. I got more agitated. I screamed "I don't know" over and over. I thought of Vicki and Val. I called Vicki. She came. I asked her what was wrong. She said, "He hurt me." I asked, "What?" Vicki said he hurt her pee-pee. Then I cried and screamed, "I want my mommy," and "Where's Mommy." I cried a long time.

You want goals, Harry? You got 'em!
1. No more swirling and escalation of my mind and emotions
2. The will to live or die—not straddle the two
3. Anger and rage resolution
4. The ability to get out of bed because I want to and not because of school or work
5. The ability to do things if I have to live—like cook, clean, sew, paint, quilt, dollhouse, write, and have a friend who is male
6. To put you in the middle of the fulcrum instead of at either end
7. To know my own boundaries—to HAVE a sense of me and my rules
8. To quit yelling at you in writing
9. To focus on that which is not me
10. To have Val & Vicki easily accessible

On a calmer note, goals of intensive treatment would be:
1. To have the freedom to feel whenever needed without the consuming intensity
2. To work the cognitive and emotion closer together
3. To relieve my mind of hidden memory
4. To give Val and Vicki freedom to come and go as they wish in hope of discovering all they know
5. Safeness to remember
6. To slow down the yo-yo fight and give whatever is inside of me a chance to get out or clear itself up in a non-threatening, no need to hide environment.

With goals in place, and insurance information gathered (I would have to pay half), I again stepped within the walls of a locked psychiatric ward. This second hospital stay was one of necessity, but not for any life-threatening reason. At least I wasn't suicidal. My brain was in such a state of confusion I had to find answers. My purpose in requesting this hospitalization was to do just that. I really needed to find out what was going on with me. I also wanted answers in regard to the sexual abuse. This hospital stay was to include psychiatric testing and interviews.

Life during this hospital stay was very different from my first hospital experience. We as a group of patients formed strong bonds for the duration of our stay. Some relationships have lasted beyond the walls of the hospital.

Every morning after breakfast and before group, several of us patients would hold Bible study. Hallie had a list of feeling words and Bible verses covering those feelings. We would choose a feeling word and look up verses with that word in it. This Bible study did a world of good for us patients. It irritated the nurses and staff. They weren't used to patients forming such a bond and were certain we were planning a revolt of some sort. One counselor even brought the counselors' fears up in group. They simply didn't believe the Bible was the focal point of our daily gathering.

Tilex. We called the nurses Tilex. They were there to scrub the mold and mildew off us patients so we could go back into the world to collect more. At least that was our perspective. Our supposed craziness would never end. You might see light at the end of the tunnel, but that light never got any closer. Hope was a word without event, thought without action. Hope was not reality.

Why were we in the hospital anyway? Weren't they suppose to find out what's wrong? Weren't they suppose to fix us?

Again, I realized that no matter how enraged or depressed one was upon entering the hospital, there was always that sense of relief. Finally, I can rest. Finally, there will be some safeness. Finally, I can act the way I have to or want to because being is okay in here. Finally, I might be fixed. Finally.

In reality, hospitals don't make promises of any sort. They take away seemingly innocuous belongings such as razor blades, mouthwash, and shoe strings. Okay, so the razor blades aren't so innocuous. But, the #1 rule in any psychiatric hospital is "Thou shalt not hurt thyself or others." Therefore, hospital personnel take away anything perceived as possible suicide instruments. During this "stealing" process, which happens at check-in, you feel invaded and relieved. Invaded because they won't let you keep your stuff. Relieved because finally somebody is helping you take care of yourself. "Take all my stuff. See if I care." Perhaps it is angry relief.

Lili wouldn't sleep in her bed. The night nurse would have to search the room for her to make sure she was present and alive. Sometimes Lili would curl up in the shower. Sometimes beneath the bathroom sink. Perhaps she could be found curled up in a ball in the darkest corner behind the bed. The bed was simply too dangerous. That man might come. The body memories might reenact various sexual experiences, experiences Lili didn't even remember. Others remembered for her. So she thought. After several days, Lili agreed to sleep in the doorway of her room if she could not sleep in her bed. It was a compromise of sorts, but at least, Lili thought, she didn't have to sleep in that bed. The body memories were as invasive as the hell of reality. Only who knew what constituted reality?

Then came the roommate. Flash floods of emotion rushed through Lili as bedtime approached. "NO! I can't sleep in that room with someone else in there. NO!" Lili fretted, sweated, and paced with furious fear volcanically erupting within her. Faster and faster the noise and the swirls burbled inside her. The pacing speed increased step by step. "I will NOT sleep in that room with *that* girl in there!" The nurses pleaded and cajoled. They tried sweet-talking and threats, firmness and bribes. Lili, however, would have none of it. She would sleep on a couch in the lounge before she would sleep in the same room as monster girl. When bedtime arrived, Lili stripped her bed and turned a love seat into a bed. "You will drop to level one" was the threat made and followed through, "Your privileges will be gone."

So what was it that made so great a threat in having a roommate? Lili feared experiencing the body memories in the presence of "that crazy noisy girl" Jolie was her name. Crazy was her game. Jolie had *real* memories, whereas, those of Lili were unknown. It was so unfair. Lili couldn't even do crazy right.

Fourteen

Here, in this safe, hopeful place, I would meet two memorable mental healthcare providers: Mandy and Dr. Keyes. Mandy was a licensed clinical social worker. Dr. Keyes was a psychiatrist. Both people brought changes that would change my mental health path.

Mandy was a beautiful woman with a beautiful spirit. She had a gentle soothing nature. And she listened. I think I fell in love with her. Mandy's spirit was that of a nurturing type. She made the abnormal okay to be. She could soothe the restless spirit as no one else had. And, again, she listened. Mandy was able to offer the reassurance that things would get better when no one else could. She had me almost believing.

Dr. Keyes was a good psychiatrist. He was personable, concerned, and honest. I liked him. When I got the hospital bill, he had only charged for the time he actually spent with me or at the staffings about me. Dr. Keyes would experiment a bit with medication and discover an antidepressant that seemed to help me. He was easy to talk to in his cowboy boots and south-western accent.

One of my hopeful goals for this hospital "visit" was to remember everything there was about the sexual abuse, most specifically the perpetrator's identity.

Dr. Keyes told me I will not remember while I am here. He was very definite and adamant. "You will not remember while you are here." He repeated himself. He meant it.

And now I have just come out of the bathroom. I took my covers with me and wept. I want to remember while here. I want the truth to come while I am in a safe environment. I want the can of worms opened. It's going to open anyway. I'd rather it opened here with days to recoup than at Harry's office with minutes to recoup. Don't they understand? I need safety to remember. I need safety for Val and Vicki to talk. I WANT TO REMEMBER!

And who is this doctor to tell me I won't. Is he stating a fact or something they decided at staffing? I want to know. I didn't realize until I came to bed how strongly this is on my agenda. I also forgot that hospitals have their own agenda. I should have been invited to my staffing.

I want to scream.

With his words, Dr. Keyes smashed my hopes of relief. My questions would not be answered. The tension would continue to build. Would nothing positive come?

The lady had a real soft voice. She had me do lots of things. The inkblots scared me. I kept seeing blood and sex stuff. That surprised me. I expected to see butterflies and caterpillars. I really don't feel like writing this. The hypnosis was good though. Vicki did not know what a hospital was. I wanted to laugh at her. Mandy later reminded me that Vicki is very young. She may not know what a hospital is. My mind wearies. And the swirling begins. I must stop.

Perhaps Mandy interpreted what she heard from me as what she was expecting, but she listened. Not only did Mandy listen, she explained, she reassured, and she read me stories. Okay, she didn't actually read stories. She gave me one story to read, ponder, and discuss. It was a Multiple Personality Disorder fairy tale. Yes, Mandy had determined that I had what was then commonly known as MPD.

She came to this diagnosis via a combination of what I told her and a hypnosis session or two. We both knew I had been dissociating (separating myself from the real world) and I think we led ourselves into expecting MPD. I wanted answers for my craziness. Mandy held a possible answer that could lead to a solution. I sometimes wonder if I made things appear the way Mandy was expecting them to look. Was I even clearheaded enough to do such a thing? At other times, I wonder if Mandy had unconsciously decided in advance the diagnosis she would bestow upon me. In the end, it doesn't matter because her diagnosis opened the door for healing.

As she looked into
my window
She told me what
she saw

PARTS OF ME
I think.

A house so filled
with mirrors
Her voice was filled
with awe

And then she shared
with me
The wonders of
them all

For each and every
mirror
was the gift of life
from God

A gift said she and strength
to come
When all these mirrors
blend into one.

Mandy did good things with me. She gave me resources within myself. She used my ability to visualize and my need for internal organization.

First, she helped me develop a locked safe in my head to hold my confusion and pain. Next, there was a beautifully carpeted spiral staircase to descend slowly while experiencing the smooth cool silver handrail under my hand and the luxurious, soft, and cozy, plushness of the carpet between my toes. At the bottom of the staircase, I turned left into a hallway with an elevator at the end and a door on the right hand side. She led me first through the door into a safe room where all the people inside me could just be. Everybody inside me found a spot to sit on or lay on or curl up in. They all seemed so relaxed and at home. There was no noise, just peaceful quietness and sometimes a feeling of playful relief.

After the night I refused to stay in my room, Mandy led me through hypnosis to the elevator at the end of the hall. The elevator led to a basement where there was a freezer waiting. I remember being in the elevator. It felt round. A ficus tree grew in the corner. When the elevator stopped, the doors opened and before me was a long gray hallway. I walked down the hall and at the end on the left was a short foyer. There was a fur coat on a hook waiting for me. I wrapped myself in the fur coat and entered the freezer. There was a block of ice in the center of the freezer. I sat down upon it. Soon, Mandy's soothing voice led all the terrible memories out of my head and into a frozen state to remain until I felt safe enough to bring them out to be dealt with and explored. It was amazing how much more peaceful I felt after my journey to the basement freezer. All the bad stuff inside me could be stored in this freezer until I felt safe enough to bring it out.

Mandy was marvelous, a good memory to have. She couldn't, however, be my therapist outside the hospital. And, oh, how I wanted her reassuring, mother-like, spirit to be my therapist if I ever lost Harry. Still, even I had to admit that a six-hour drive each week (one way) would be a bit much. Just the thought of her brightens my mind.

I miss you, Mandy.

Fifteen

Harry dumped me. With the diagnosis of Multiple Personality Disorder, he decided to dump me. I knew at some level that Harry did not have the skills to deal with my emotional garbage. I knew he would refer me to someone else, though "refer" was not the word my head used. My head used such words as "dumped," "kicked out," "abandoned," "dropped." You know, words more aggressive and dismal than the bland "refer." Sure, it was for my own good, but I was pissed.

On today: Some of the fun will end tonight—I mean this afternoon—when I see Harry. I dread the words to come forth from his mouth. It makes me want to cry even as I write. Harry is the first person to let me be me. He corrects me or tells me I am being irrational, but he still allows me to be. I can "yell" at him. I can write angry things to him, and it's okay. We frustrate each other and laugh together. He prays for me. I don't want to lose him. I really truly don't. I am crying. Painful tears.

Later: Well, Harry isn't tossing me out the door. At least not yet. He is working on finding someone to work with me from the dissociative aspect, and will or will not work with me according to the therapist I end up with. We aren't meeting again until the data from the hospital arrives.

I told Harry that he is like the maid who says, "I don't do windows." Only he says, "I don't do dissociatives." He roared with laughter and stated that the difference was a maid has the capability to do windows. I offered to be the guinea pig. I offered to blow the dust off his hypnotherapist certificate for him. He declined the offer. Then I suggested that perhaps God would perform a miracle and sprinkle upon him and through him all the knowledge and ability needed to work with dissociatives. He ignored that one. Yes, our relationship is back to normal. I yelled once, and Harry laughed. I tried to explain to him why he is so important. I don't know that I explained it at all well. C'est la vie. (I think.)

I had trusted Harry. His office was a place of safeness where any words coming out of my mouth were accepted. Questions were answered. Any ignorance was okay. Even though I was getting worse instead of better while seeing Harry, my psyche had latched onto his soothing calming nature. His office afforded a peacefulness not found elsewhere in my day-to-day living. For one hour a week, I could sit in an oasis of peace. My own being continued to be wrecked with havoc, but the internal peace I craved could be glimpsed at externally in Harry's office.

My relationship with Harry consisted of that longing to be understood and the desire to find my me. He was allowed to see bits of me no one else saw — that deep dark terribleness of me had started leaking out for Harry to see.

Thinking about it, I believe my relationship with Harry was a test of trust. What would he do if he discovered how horrible my insides were? Well, now I found out. He was dumping me.

I had put all my trust in Harry, and in the end, he failed that trust. As a therapist Harry did everything as he ought. He sought help in figuring me out. He maintained a calm persona no matter what my manner. And he made the most ethical move he could when it became obvious that he did not have the necessary skills to work with me. Harry referred me elsewhere. I have often wondered what he would have done if I had refused to leave.

In my mind I knew that Harry was doing what he should do, sort of. Harry was looking out for what he thought was my best interest. In my search for love I could not comprehend that this referral was an act of love and in my best interest. I interpreted this move as abandonment and rejection. My greatest fear had been realized. Someone had seen some of my darkness and that someone had rejected me. Such was the beginning of my ugliest, darkest, and loudest raging lamentations.

Change was my enemy. With the constant noise and visual confusion in my head, external real-world stability was of extreme importance. The soothing atmosphere of Harry's office had become the focal point of my week. The moment I left Harry's office, the countdown began toward the next appointment time. When Harry would change the appointment time, I would freak out. The rhythmic cadence of appointments became out of sync — and believe me, I have never been able to play syncopated music. The beat must be steady, equal, staid. Imagine singing "Mary had a little" and not saying "lamb" until two beats later. Try it, I will bet your head still says lamb on the appointed beat even if your lips do not. When Harry rejected me (I know, I know, referred me) my head had nowhere to put me, no rhythm to follow until the next session. I was at a loss without the familiar weekly pattern. The "lamb" was missing, yet my head kept screaming out for it. I was horrified at the thought of trusting someone new. I was not to trust for a very long time.

The new therapist was not Harry. The new therapist wore above-the-knee skirts. The new therapist kept trying to get me to look at her and put my feet on the ground. The new therapist kept looking at me, smiling. The new therapist would not answer my questions. I had no place for her in my crowded head. The new therapist was named Hannah Lee.

I hated the idea of her. It meant I was a failure with Harry. I could be rejected and sent away. Again. There became no such thing as trust. None.

I wanted Harry. I wanted Mandy. I needed Hannah Lee.

Nine Long Years

Even youths grow tired and weary,
and young men stumble and fall;
but those who hope in the Lord
will renew their strength.
They will soar on wings like eagles;
they will run and not grow weary,
they will walk and not be faint.

Isaiah 40:30-31

Sixteen

Hannah Lee, P-H-D
Makes me want
to hide and flee,
Hannah Lee P-H-D
You'd best take
good care of me.

My first steps toward Hannah Lee's office were hesitant and fearful. Everything was different from Harry's from the moment I walked into the waiting area. First of all there was no cheerfully pleasant receptionist to greet me and make me feel welcome and comfortable. In fact, there wasn't even a window for a receptionist to greet me from if there'd even been a receptionist. All the furniture was the wrong color and not in the right place. There were couches, and the chairs were too close together. There was nowhere to hide. No nooks. No crannies. No receptionist. I was quite disgusted. How was Hannah Lee to know I was there awaiting her care and protection? The whole setup irked me.

Then out came Hannah Lee—pert and cute in a professional way. She smiled and twinkled a greeting. She terrified me. Oh, how I resented being in her office.

This first session was supposed to be a trial to see whether I would get along with Hannah Lee. She presented her credentials. I sat there shaking, feeling as if none of this were real. I felt as if I were in a protective bubble and could not touch the office around me. Hannah Lee had a corner office where two walls were windows. I had to admit it was a glorious view filled with sky and clouds. I would spend many an hour discovering horses and angels and bears within the clouds. Hannah Lee felt that such visions were not therapy. I disagreed. The pictures in the clouds soothed my spirit. Yes, my sightings were a diversion, but not a total avoidance of myself and my therapy. It was partly a way to calm and soothe myself and find clarity of thought along with some courage to share the discombobulated workings of my head.

First Impressions [4]

Lili's initial appointment was on September 28, 1993. She was thirty-six years old and had been seeing her previous therapist for two and one half years. Her goal for therapy during this time had been "not crying all the time." Her therapist had referred her to me because she had been diagnosed during a recent hospital stay as suffering from Multiple Personality Disorder.

Lili had a number of strengths. She was a special education teacher. She was in a graduate program in counseling, about which she informed me, "I started it. I'm going to finish it. No one's going to stop me." She was active in a church, and had a positive relationship with a younger sister. She also had positive relationships with two previous therapists.

On the other side of the coin, Lili described a number of difficulties that would need to be addressed in therapy. There was, of course, the previously mentioned "crying all the time". She said she tended to "fog out" and described several "alter personalities". She had two previous hospitalizations and an incident with a rotary cutter, which resulted in police and paramedics being called.

The discharge summary from Lili's second hospitalization stated, "It became clear ... that she in fact was an MPD." The document described a recent loss of relationship resulting in the onset of depression; memories and flashbacks of abuse; a history of suicidality and self-harm; and experiencing fragmented parts of herself as separate personalities. The report concluded, "It will be important that her therapy focus specifically on the Multiple Personality Disorder."

From the beginning of our work together, I noted a number of red flags related to the diagnosis of MPD (or Dissociative Identity Disorder, as it would come to be known). First of all, there were no visible signs of switching from one personality to another. This was unusual given the anxiety about meeting a new therapist at intake. Even more unusual, there was no visible sign of switching over a period of weeks and months, even when Lili was enraged at me (as she often was).

4   Each titled section has been written by Dr. Cheryl Arnold, aka Hannah Lee.

Another red flag was Lili's familiarity with the description of the MPD diagnosis, and her being encouraged to read technical material on the diagnosis. It often seemed that she wanted me to tell her how to be MPD. She wanted me to hypnotize her and call the various alter personalities out. She wanted me to control her, and she wanted to control me.

A third red flag was Lili's lack of ability to discriminate between real and not real. While she went back and forth in believing that she was sexually violated, she indicated that her inpatient therapist "flat out stated that it happened".

Rather than focussing specifically on the MPD diagnosis, I decided that the initial goals of therapy would be establishing a therapeutic alliance and an ongoing evaluation of Lili. I was determined to treat the person, not just a diagnosis.

• •

Hannah Lee's therapy hour was a strict forty-five minutes. She showed me right away that boundaries were expected to be present and respected. Her boundaries felt like an immovable steel wall. Don't ask personal questions. Leave when forty-five minutes are up. Do therapy. Sit up. Look at her. The list went on. I ignored her rules as much as possible. Partly because I wanted to. Partly because I was so needy in my mind's eye. I needed her time and lots of it. I needed to know all about Hannah Lee so I could know myself. I didn't want therapy; I wanted to be held and relieved. On and on my rather selfish reasons ran.

Hannah Lee presented herself in a very professional manner with boundaries of steel. She was top in her field. She was even on TV once or twice! Hannah Lee insisted that only matters therapeutic in nature were to be discussed in her office. We did not always agree on what was considered therapeutic. I was not allowed to know anything personal about her for a very long time. As our relationship evolved, I came to respect Hannah Lee, and to love her. She has a great sense of humor and an exuberance for life. We share many common interests. I would love to become friends with her, but she would say, "That's not ethical."

Hannah Lee seemed to love change. Her hair changed so much it scared me. Every time she changed her hair, I had to find a new picture to put in my head. It was very confusing. Yet, Hannah Lee would be the gift from God who would help me eventually find my me.

During my first two years with Hannah Lee, I was in a constant state of rage. Any anger that had ever existed within me snowballed into one gigantic rage directed at Hannah Lee. I envisioned stabbing her and slicing her guts up over and over. The scenario always had her dead and me safe. No one would ever know it was I who had killed her. I would take a shower and be safe from detection. If I killed Hannah Lee, I could go back to Harry and be happily in denial. I drew pictures of drowning Hannah Lee, of slicing her guts out. Never had there existed such an all consuming rage.

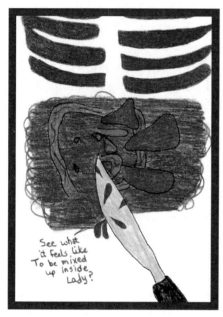

See what it feels like To be mixed up inside, Lady?

Where did all this raging anger come from? It seemed the years of stuffing and hiding anger finally reached its peak and decided to explode. Once begun, the angry rage just kept building and flowing. It seemed that finally the anger had stretched its skin to a point beyond return. Hence the explosion. That had always been one of my fears, that I would explode into pieces if I ever got angry.

Hannah Lee made a comment on Thursday. I heard only two parts. "You are afraid of your anger," and "Anger doesn't have to be destructive." I don't know if there was anything between those two statements. It does seem that she is inferring that I am afraid of my anger because I believe anger is destructive. Why didn't she ever tell me this before? I can see where I would have that belief about anger. I think she is right. Why hasn't she told me how anger can be resolved without being destructive? If she knew all this why didn't she ever tell me this before?

My head held all sorts of reasons to fear anger. Anger caused bruises. Bruises of the body. Bruises of the heart and spirit. Anger was dangerous because it could put holes in walls or ignore the pleadings of the heart.

The dead therapist

Anger made people go away and never come back. Anger caused explosions with fireworks everywhere. My head held anger upon a very tall pedestal of fear. High enough to be out of reach. High enough to avoid. High enough to be safe. Almost safe. The pedestal of fear held all the anger I had ever witnessed and all the anger I had ever held. Then the unthinkable happened. The pedestal toppled, and I toppled with it. I was surrounded by all the anger and rage it held. I don't think that at first I recognized that enormous amount of anger surrounding me. All I knew was that it was loud and dangerous, and that I was spiraling downward with tornado-like fury engulfed with both the anger and the fear. I must say it was a rather pessimistic time for me. I kept waiting for Dorothy's house to fall upon me as it did upon the wicked witch in the land of Oz; for in a way, I was already in my own land of Oz. I certainly wasn't in Kansas anymore!

Hannah Lee was forever telling me I wouldn't explode, that I hadn't exploded. The real part of me knew she was right. The crazy part of me knew I was right.

On a recent night, I had a jarring encounter with anger. A remake of "Carrie" was on television. I had never seen the original, but was curious about what little I knew—the bucket of pig blood dumped on the prom queen. I watched the movie becoming rather disappointed with it. I was determined to see it through because of all the hype. Finally, the bucket of blood was dumped. Then all my fears of anger became visibly real. Carrie froze with emotion which I deemed to be anger and possibly fear. She just stood there staring into space stiff from head to toe. As she stood there, the world around her began to spark, move, crumble, drop. Doors locked themselves, lights exploded—chaos took hold as Carrie's anger throbbed and thrived with its torment. The scene was horrific. Then, suddenly, like Frankenstein's monster in a trance, Carrie began walking. She left the building. As she walked, the world around her exploded and shattered and caught fire. I watched in amazement as all my fears of anger happened right before my very eyes. The exciting moment was when I looked at all the exploding and noticed two things. First, Carrie herself did not blow up into little pieces. Whew! The second thing I noticed was that it wasn't real. Watching Carrie taking her slow journey through the high school and town with her anger destroying everything and everyone in sight was not real. It could not really happen that way. Yes, anger can be hurtful, and physical or emotional damage can be a result of anger, but anger will not spontaneously blow the world, or me, up. Thank you, Carrie.

Emotions have often been a strange bird to me. I knew how to laugh and smile, but admitting or recognizing anything else was a mystery. When Hannah Lee came on the scene, the whirlpool of intensely overwhelming emotion took over my being. I did not know what to do with this magnitude of emotion, yet managed to imagine and do quite a bit with it anyway.

IN THE BEGINNING

I find Lili's description of the beginning of our work together interesting. She first lays out for the reader her feelings of abandonment when Harry referred her to me, then describes the boundaries established in therapy. These quickly moved her into her rage and anger at me.

I have to admit, sometimes being a therapist can be uncomfortable. It was uncomfortable seeing Lili's image of stabbing me and slicing my guts up. This is an example of a time when truly understanding Lili was essential to our work in therapy being productive. If I had responded to her rage with fear, it would have reinforced her belief that anger and rage were unacceptable and dangerous. If I had not recognized the intensity of her rage, she might have had to act it out to convince me of its power.

The issues related to Lili's rage that begged understanding were abandonment and boundaries. The issue of abandonment struck terror in her heart. She felt confused and out of control, and feared that no one would be able to help her. She had felt hopeful working with Mandy, but when she was discharged from the hospital Mandy was gone. She had begun to share her "terrible darkness" with Harry, and Harry had "dumped" her. She was enraged at me for taking Harry's place, yet was terrified I, too, would "dump" her. In my case, it was complicated. My leaving her was both her wish (so she could go back to Harry) and her fear (her terror, really, of being abandoned and alone).

The issue of clear boundaries further complicated Lili's fear of abandonment. She hoped for a merger with me, not a relationship. How can you have a relationship with another person when you don't have a self? Lili felt out of control and unable to control herself. A merger would ensure that I would take control and keep her safe. On the other hand, if I refused to merge or to allow her to control me, how could she be certain I wouldn't leave her? The only reasonable solution was, of course, trust. But trust, initially, was impossible. Trust would take a long time and a great deal of consistency to develop.

· ·

Seventeen

I would laugh when other people stomped their feet or yelled. For a long time, I felt no anger at all. I simply laughed and meant it. During my second hospital stay, Hallie, another patient, would enjoy my so-called rampages of laughter. The most memorable one dealt with brown sugar. The cafeteria did not send the requested brown sugar with my oatmeal. This had happened more than once. Well, finally I was fed up. What did I do? I laughed. I ranted and raved about the matter, laughing all the while. Expression of anger was not my thing. I didn't become angry in front of people easily if at all.

Although anger had taken over my brain, expressing this anger to Hannah Lee was very difficult. I certainly had no clue as to how to deal with anger in an appropriate, useful, and acceptable manner. In my head there was a fragmented one called The Gray and White One. I came to fear The Gray and White One. The things this fragment was writing!

Hannah Lee has me all confused. Hannah Lee says I was already confused; she just brought it to my attention. I am not allowed to call her or write to her this week. I don't know whether she means me, The Gray and White One, or both of us. Hannah Lee insists we are one and the same, so she must mean both of us. She says I said and wrote bad things to her. She said I attacked her. Hannah Lee wouldn't talk. She said she wouldn't talk because no matter what she said, I would say it was wrong. I got on this kick of wanting to know whether she tells everybody the same things she tells me. She wanted me to admit that all of my mes are just me. I am supposed to embrace and listen to all my inside pieces. I am to accept the fact that we are all one me. I am supposed to say that only one person can live in a body and a mind. She says all my parts are just feelings and that they are my feelings.

DEALING WITH FEELINGS

The first requirement of therapy is always safety. In order to establish safety, a distinction must be made between feelings and behaviors. Feeling murderous rage is acceptable. Acting on it is not. We (I) talked a lot about the difference in feelings and behaviors. While feelings are always acceptable in therapy, destructive behaviors are not. I was very clear with Lili that I expected her to control her behaviors. If she was unable to do so, she was to contact me. Together we would make a plan to provide as much structure as she needed to stay safe, up to and including hospitalization.

Refusing to buy into Lili's "merger fantasy" allowed me to pay attention to my own feelings in response to hers, and to use those feelings to gain a deeper understanding of Lili. My twinge of discomfort and apprehension in response to Lili's rage communicated to me that beneath the rage she was feeling and expressing was a reservoir of fear. Her fear of her emotions prevented her from dealing with them productively.

While Lili knew in her head that she was angry, she did not allow herself to feel the anger. If she felt it, she might explode. If she felt it, she might hurt herself or someone else. So, for a long time, Lili felt no anger at all. She defended against it with humor. This solution, however, was not effective forever. The time came when Lili had to develop a more powerful way of managing her rage and anger.

She did so through dissociating. Dissociation is a defense in which one can split off unacceptable aspects of oneself (such as anger) and experience them as external to one's self. When Lili's rage and anger became intolerable, she split them off into "The Gray and White One". The Gray and White One was not sufficiently elaborated to be considered an alter personality. However, this split off part did allow Lili to continue to distance herself from the feelings she found unacceptable while clearly communicating them to me through the U.S. postal service.

I responded to this turn of events by sharing the letters received from The Gray and White One with Lili during therapy sessions. We had quite a process going on: she would split off her anger; The Gray and White One would express it in written form and mail it to me; I would then share it with Lili. This procedure allowed her to gradually become conscious of her feelings, allowing her to make conscious choices to deal productively with the feelings in a safe and contained environment. As she began to recognize her feelings, she developed an ability to process them in pictures and in words. She came to accept the feelings as a part of being human, and to integrate previously unacceptable feelings as a part of her self.

· ·

The Gray and White One did not have a vocal voice. I saw only flashes of the colors gray and white when The Gray and White One was busy.

Furtively the pencil etched its way across the paper. She was mad, really mad. That Hannah Lee lady was ugly, so ugly. And she was mean. Rage filled the girl who wrote in childish block letters. She used the pencil as a ferocious weapon lancing the pain of rage, allowing the pent up feelings an escape.

The letters to Hannah Lee contained words of fury, words of hate. The letters were always mailed to Hannah Lee. Hannah Lee didn't like them. She insisted those ugly letters were written by me, but I knew nothing about them. At least not directly. I would remember only swirls of gray and white in motion. Hannah Lee would hand the letters to me and tell me to read them. I couldn't do it. The letters scared me. They expressed an intense rage I denied. The letters represented a part of me with which I was unfamiliar. I insisted someone else wrote the nasty, hor-

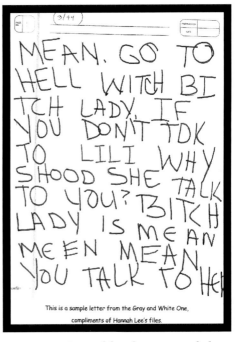

This is a sample letter from the Gray and White One, compliments of Hannah Lee's files.

rid, angry letters. "It wasn't me!" was my cry. I would refuse to read them because I couldn't say those words; they were words I never even thought. Why should I read something I hadn't written? Hannah Lee would gently disagree. "I see only one person," she would say. "There is only one of you. Allow yourself to know your parts." Hannah Lee was always like that. She didn't believe in all the people I claimed to have inside of me. She believed that was how I experienced myself, but Hannah Lee insisted always that there was only one me. I ignored her opinion and angrily denied I ever wrote such words. "Ah, but you did write them," Hannah Lee would say. She would then proceed to read the letters to me, and I would disappear.

Even now, while I know she was right, I deny that I ever wrote those letters. I don't talk or think that way. I really don't. I don't know how long The Gray and White One wrote those letters. Months or years, I don't know. My space-time continuum was a bit off in those days.

Besides harboring inordinate anger, for several years I was seldom totally present during therapy sessions. Considering the fact that in my head I didn't exist, this was a pretty easy state to be in. I would "fog out" to the point where I either felt as if I were asleep and later remembered nothing, or I would be aware of conversation taking place but didn't feel I was experiencing the conversation myself.

One of the reasons I was willing to see Hannah Lee had to do with hypnosis. Hannah Lee was well-trained in the use of hypnosis. Hypnosis was a soothing and relaxing experience with Mandy. From what Mandy told me, hypnosis would be the route to go to discover the so-called alters and other secrets within me. I wanted to know the secrets within me. I demanded answers between Hannah Lee and me. I cried out for answers to my innumerable questions. Hannah Lee was more concerned with the present and being able to function in current everyday life.

When Mandy used hypnosis with me, I felt as if I were in a safe protective bubble that could only be popped by me. Mandy felt strongly about the use of hypnosis. She thought it was the way to work with Multiple Personality Disorder. Hannah Lee was different. Hannah Lee's training in hypnosis didn't benefit me much. No, she wanted me to be present. "Besides," she said, "you put yourself into trances." She was right. I fogged out constantly performing tasks and holding conversations with no memory of them. Evidently, I wasn't freaking anybody out; no one complained. There was, however, some use Hannah Lee had for hypnosis.

There was a door in the safe room Mandy helped me create that led to the outside. Hannah Lee helped me create a safe place outside that door with a house and a gentle river and with trees nearby. The house was a yellow and white rambling two-story old fashioned house with a rickety comforting front porch. Here, the people inside me could laugh and breathe in joy. Sometimes God would come here and wrap me in his arms. It was a beautiful place.

Other than this one creation, Hannah Lee's use of hypnosis was limited to counting to five to help me become somewhat grounded and defragmented. Then she would count from five to one to "wake" me up ready to drive home. Yes, Hannah Lee used hypnosis sparingly.

Miss Warner was how Hannah Lee always referred to the adult me. Miss Warner was the part of me capable of functioning in the real world. Miss Warner got me through school and work with some semblance of normalcy. I never felt acquainted with Miss Warner. That responsible adult seemed foreign to me. I wanted to be taken care of. I wanted to curl up with Hannah Lee in the rocking chair and suck my thumb. I wanted her to rock me forever in her comforting lap. Meanwhile, Hannah Lee would call for Miss Warner and try to get me to put my feet on the floor and look at her. Hannah Lee strongly believed a person should keep his or her feet on the floor. Somehow that was supposed to keep a person more grounded in the present. Perhaps she was right. I wouldn't know; my feet were seldom on the floor.

Where were my feet? On the couch, of course. I always sat lengthwise on the couch and covered myself with pillows to protect myself from Hannah Lee and what was to come. My eyes and mind and ears dodged hither and yon discovering all sorts of interesting things. I would see faces in the ceiling dots; I'd look for pictures in the clouds. I would ask Hannah Lee a zillion personal questions only to be thwarted by her concrete boundaries. She didn't seem to get my need to have a picture and place for her in my head. She was an abstract in my life I was trying to transform into a concrete picture in my head. Hannah Lee said I was being voyeuristic. I just needed a place to put her. Perhaps the lack of organization within my brain needed some sort of organized space for Hannah Lee so I could always find her.

While I tended to appear cheerful, I don't know whether I was or not. I laughed a lot, and smiled, and appeared interested in what was going on around me. On the other hand, I was almost always seeing visions of hurting myself. Generally, the pictures were of ripping my face off with my fingernails. I would drag the flesh into hanging strips of bloody tinsel. In my visions, my face would become unrecognizable. Of course, they were only visions. In reality, I didn't know what to do with my anger. My internal anger was so very violent that it frightened me. This may explain my oddly timed laughter. If I didn't laugh, who was I going to hurt? I wished for all my anger to go away so I would not hurt anybody. Hannah Lee said it was safe to be angry in her office. I didn't know about that. Besides, Hannah Lee wouldn't tell me how to be angry, or if she did, I didn't hear her.

The vengeful anger encompassed me. Since there was no me inside of me, there was plenty of room for the anger to balloon into and fill. My body was in constant pain from the tension. I was drawing constantly, frantically, to get rid of the anger. Hannah Lee bore the brunt of my anger. She seldom complained though did on occasion make comments about it. One time, Hannah Lee gave me a homework assignment to paint or draw my anger. I got this huge old foam board and went at it. It was filled with great splashes of red and yellow on a rather depressing dull green and black background. At least that is how I remember it. After showing the picture to Hannah Lee, I was afraid of it and asked if it could stay in her office. For the next eight and a half years, my anger painting stayed in Hannah Lee's office behind shelves. When she moved to a different office across town, the painting went, too. I never looked at it again. I was afraid of the powerful anger it represented. My head would play games with me and scare me whenever I envisioned the picture in my head. At our last session Hannah Lee asked me if I wanted the picture. Fear pounded through my heart as I looked for an escape. Simply though, I said, "No, I don't want it," and that was that. I don't know where it is now. She probably threw it away. Why would she want my anger when I didn't want it myself?

I never looked at Hannah Lee. To do so would have exposed all there was to hide. I knew that if anyone made eye contact with me they would see everything inside me. And there was so much to hide and hide from. If Hannah Lee saw inside me, she might make me see all the horror within me. I wish I could explain that horror of darkness, but it was so dark and dense with fright, I was not even certain what it was. It was as if I were in an art museum faced with a painting I could not decipher. All I knew for certain, was that there was a dark terribleness inside me that I had to hide from everyone, myself included. Especially myself.

It is amazing what our minds can do. Mine, for several years, could not separate real from not-real. I could not tell the difference between my internal world and the external world. Frankly, I didn't experience myself as having an inner world and an outer world. I had no skill at distinguishing between the two; they were but one world and reality to me.

Hannah Lee kept telling me that I had fantasies. I just didn't believe her. "How could she argue such hogwash?" I didn't believe her because in my experience the mesh between internal and external became a singular unit. *My* reality was what many in the world would consider nuts. Yet, it was my normal everyday world.

Eventually, I began to forgive Hannah Lee for taking over from Harry. It took years before the anger totally dissolved and was close to three years before I would admit that perhaps I wasn't so resentful and perhaps didn't really hate her. What a process!

GROUNDED IN REALITY

An important aspect of working with Lili was that of evaluating ego strength and providing therapeutic interventions that would increase ego strength versus contributing to her fragmentation and regression.

Reality testing was an area of difficulty for Lili. It was clear that she did not have an accurate sense of internal versus external events. Her lack of boundaries prevented her from distinguishing events that happened (objective reality) from those that she imagined or dreamed (subjective reality). In my opinion, this was reason enough not to pursue "traumatic memories", especially through hypnosis.

Lili's sense of reality was impaired by her ability to "fog out". A cohesive sense of self was nonexistent. She experienced depersonalization, feeling that she was not real. She had no sense of agency. For example, when her hand hit her head during session, it "just happened". She did not believe that she had any control over her actions. At times, Lili described being aware of conversation taking place but did not feel that she actually experienced it herself. She experienced derealization, feeling that the world around her was unreal. Finally, Lili's orientation to time and space was problematic. In her words, "my space-time continuum was a bit off in those days".

Given her deficits in ego functioning, Lili is absolutely correct that I was more concerned with the present and her being able to function than I was with gratifying her desire to "discover the so-called alters and other secrets" she believed were lurking inside of her. From my perspective, I did not believe I could determine the reality of Lili having experienced abuse if she herself could not distinguish between reality and fantasy.

From her previous experiences in therapy, Lili came to me with the expectation that (1) she was suffering from Multiple Personality Disorder, and (2) the treatment of choice for her condition was hypnosis. She had experienced symbiotic (or merger) relationships with her previous two therapists. She felt "one with" Harry due to her perception of sameness through religion. She experienced a sense of merger with Mandy due to her sense that Mandy knew and understood her better than she knew herself. She defined her self through Mandy's diagnosis of Multiple Personality Disorder. When I thwarted her expectations of me in these areas, she had no idea of what to do with me or how to develop a relationship with me. These circumstances somewhat dictated what Lili would be able to tolerate in our initial work together.

She wanted (demanded) hypnosis. While I refused to utilize hypnosis regressively, I did believe it was appropriate to utilize hypnosis for ego strengthening. Thus, we created a safe place inside to help Lili feel less anxious and more in control of her life. While I saw little evidence of alter personalities, utilizing "MPD language" was useful in encouraging Lili to be her adult self. Asking "Miss Warner" to take responsibility was a way of encouraging Lili to function appropriately at home, at school, at work, and in therapy.

• •

Eighteen

After the angry rage began calming down, I was ready to spiral downward a few more times. The spring before my summer of noise, I had begun graduate school studying what else, but psychology and counseling! Talk about an oxymoron—the nut case studying nuts. (Please note that I am at liberty to use such a phrase as I am jesting about myself.) Going to school was difficult. Studying the different aspects of psychology was, at times, nearly impossible. In studying psychology, one must be willing to look at one's self. But, I didn't believe I had a self so how could I look at my self?

There were so many days when I could barely focus on classes. The noise in my head often spoke louder than the professor. I was often unable to separate the words of the professor from the words in my head.

Then there were the ISSUES.

Human Sexuality, a required course, was taught by a man. Because of the supposed sexual molestation and the body memories, I was terrified of this course. We'd have to talk about body parts and functions and stuff. We would have to look at pictures! Forcing myself to sit through this class has to have been one of the hardest things I have ever done. My head would be swirling with pictures and angst. Frequently I would call Hannah Lee during breaks. I would page her with the phone number and stay glued to the pay phone until she called back. I would be all jumbled up inside ready to cry. Val would cry. Vicki would yell, scream, and stomp her foot. I would be all jittery, unable to focus. Hannah Lee would count to five and back to help calm me down. Then I would return to class and more torture.

LIFE CHOICES

You may wonder why I allowed Lili to enroll in a psychology class (much less a class on sexuality) given her emotional and mental state. The answer is twofold: she chose to do so, and I believe people usually know what is right for themselves.

Lili's life choices belong to *her*. In order to honor the reality that it was Lili's right and responsibility to run her life, just as it was my right to run my own, it was essential for me to support her in taking responsibility for her choices. You may recall that regarding graduate school, Lili had already told me, "I started it. I'm going to finish it. No one's going to stop me." That is a life affirming choice! It indicated that she planned to live long enough to see it through.

Being in graduate school provided additional structure for Lili's life and grounded her in present-day objective reality. School required her to reality test and to recognize a shared reality with other adults. It required her to use her considerable intelligence in a positive way.

School also resulted in additional opportunities for us to evaluate together whether Lili had been sexually abused. She stated that her fear of the Human Sexuality class was based on "the supposed sexual molestation and the body memories." Her words indicate her own doubt as to the veracity of the molestation. When an abuse victim shares their abuse history, it is important to listen and to believe what they say. However, when a client speculates that he or she *may* have been abused, it is not the therapist's place to make a final determination nor to convince the client of that reality. In this instance, it was important to believe what Lili was saying: she could not distinguish between what was real or not-real.

When in class, Lili experienced confusion and noise in her head. The sexual material was not triggering specific memories nor did it result in Lili elaborating on the sexual memories she had reported three years earlier as I would have anticipated had she experienced sexual trauma. The reality was that when she was able to calm down, she was also able to deal with the sexual content of the class in a fairly objective manner.

* *

Classes where we had to role play therapeutic situations were also horrible. I never volunteered to partake and said as little as possible when required to role play group therapy.

One professor told us that if we were clinically depressed, we would be unable to attend class; we'd most likely be in bed. I was taken aback because I was considered clinically depressed and I was in class. What the professor couldn't know was that it was being in grad school that kept me relatively safe during this period.

Most of my mental health paperwork identified me as "high functioning" because I gave the appearance of holding a job and I showed up for every therapy session. Being "high functioning" allowed me to continue being an effective teacher. The children brought a focus that overshadowed the shadows and noise of my brain. The children brought me outside myself. They gave me joy. I enjoyed helping them find their way through academics. For all that went on, the children did not suffer. If there had been any probability of that I would have quit.

Add to this my graduate work, and "high functioning" described me. My "high functioning" status kept me alive. Although I was not performing my duties as efficiently or as well as I might, I was going through the motions. I looked good. Again, that gift of acting normal came in mighty handy. I went through graduate school terrified the professors would find me out then kick me out.

Going to graduate school, studying counseling, helped keep me a part of the real world. I had always loved going to school, learning, and writing. Research papers were a delicious puzzle waiting to be put together. I am also very goal oriented and did my best to reach those goals. These were what made grad school a good place to be. For a period of time each week, I could live outside myself to a certain extent and focus on the world around me.

As torturous as it was sitting through those classes, those same classes allowed a bit of normalcy to dance into my brain. Attending class, doing homework, meeting deadlines all played a rather therapeutic role in my recovery. Grad school helped keep me alive by occupying my mind away from myself. On the one hand, grad school added stress to my already stressful life; on the other hand, it aided in saving it. Graduate school was important.

Nineteen

As much as I fought Hannah Lee, I longed for the peace her office and her presence held. I would have lived in Hannah Lee's office if she'd have let me. My mind often plotted out ways I could hide in her office, and she would never know. I ached for that serenity and peace.

And I am here to tell you not all offices afforded me peace or serenity. On occasion we would have to use a different office for our therapy session. (This, as I now think of it, I should have viewed as a foreshadowing of Hannah Lee becoming Ms. Famous World Traveler.)

One office was filled with floral patterns and rabbits. The room was so busy with color and design my mind couldn't take it. What little ability I had to "do therapy" disappeared in this office. We would end up in a plain dinky little room with a couple chairs and a refrigerator. I would spend much energy bemoaning the fact that we weren't in Hannah Lee's office. Change was not my friend. Hannah Lee's office was.

One way of always being in Hannah Lee's office, and a way to make sure she had to let me come back, came in the form of a small Sculpy figurine I had made. Her name was Miss Warner. She was a representation of me and kind of a protection of my place in Hannah Lee's office. Miss Warner now sits watching me write.

So much emotion was packed inside me I cannot come close to describing it all. My body was always tense waiting for its explosion and trying to keep me all together. I want to say I was like a loaded gun. The pressure on the trigger was a fragile restraint of bullets waiting to be set free. One slight provocation and the bullets of emotion would rush out of their chambers to freedom. Now the bullet may be free, but to what end? Would someone be hurt? This possibility frightened me. I could not allow myself the luxury of freeing my emotions. They might hurt somebody.

The question was: How do I deal with all this emotion and *not* hurt anybody, including myself? I don't know whether I ever found an answer to that question. Sometimes I think the bombarding emotions just disappeared. I questioned whether therapy helped calm them down or not, yet knew that without therapy I would not be. Even now I am not sure that I dealt with each and every emotion. There seems to have been a bit of that domino effect upon lowering the emotional tension. Sadness, grief, anger, rage, hurt, disappointment—it was as if in dealing with one piece of emotion, other pieces had their load lightened. Somehow, the pressure on the trigger lessened and disappeared. The bullets came out of the chamber into my hand no longer dangerous or threatening.

The therapy process is not a simple one. There may be some people for whom a few to several sessions may be plenty. However, for many more people, being in it for the long haul, i.e., several years, is a necessity. Therapy itself was a slow process for me. It was searching through pond scum one piece of scum at a time to find both the man-eating alligator and the freshwater pearls.

Hannah Lee had a beautiful gift of patience and was always able to keep her feet planted on the ground—even when she reclined the recliner a bit. I could not have been an easy client, even when the hate-filled anger calmed down and The Gray and White One's letters stopped.

Boundaries. Ugh. As I mentioned before, Hannah Lee had boundaries. I didn't. At least none of a healthy nature. Hannah Lee expected me to respect her boundaries. I didn't. I pummeled Hannah Lee with questions about herself. Where did she live? Was she married? Did she have children? Did she live in a house or an apartment? How old was she? What did she eat for lunch? Was her husband mean? How come she got divorced? On and on the questions would burst out of my mouth. With all that was going on in my head, I needed to build a place in my head for Hannah Lee to be. Asking questions about her slowed my brain a bit and gave me something to focus on besides me. Also, asking questions of Hannah Lee saved me from searching for questions for me. My so-called voyeurism gave me time.

One of the most difficult aspects about boundaries was keeping straight what was Hannah Lee and what was me. I was sort of a chameleon in that I would "be" whomever I was with. After one session, Hannah Lee gave me homework to write: "I am not Hannah Lee." I wrote it once and said, "See. I wrote it."

My perspective on therapy was one where therapy was a domain of my very own. It was the one thing that I perceived as being totally mine and belonging only to me. This was another one of those things that had ambiguity. I did not feel in control of what would happen or be said in therapy, but I claimed private secret ownership of whatever it contained. This sense of ownership did not mean I admitted everything in my head, or coming out of my mouth was me. No, ownership of therapy meant it was private. Totally and completely private. This was a significant step for me: my first conscious boundary. I was even able to express this boundary to my mother, and she respected it. What a wonderful step that was.

My long time terror of being found out didn't exist to the same extent or in the same way within the walls of therapy. Those physical concrete walls represented containment of whatever leaked out of me during the therapy sessions. Having a physical place to contain my leaks of craziness allowed my perceived ugly dark terribleness a place to be and become a part of me. The room in which therapy took place became a container to hold all that junk waiting to be dealt with, discarded, or accepted.

One part of therapy was the hope, relief, and belief that here was some-one who would take care of me. I was tired of trying to take care of myself. I wanted someone else to be responsible. Hannah Lee, I decided, was in charge of me. Her job was to coddle me, hold me, soothe me, envelop me with peace and love and understanding. I saw her as the holder and care-taker of my pain.

Hannah Lee was the adult in charge. She pretty much disagreed with my philosophy and was rather insistent that she was merely a bit of support and not my keeper. This, of course, was a bone of contention between us. I tried to drag her into my fantasy. She insisted upon being a therapist and sidestepped my every move. Yet in many ways Hannah Lee did take care of me. Not in the way I wished for or anticipated, but in her boundaried therapeutic way.

HANNAH LEE AND
BABY ME.

She was across the country on one of her early "famous travels" when my bird died. I freaked out. For some rea-son, my dead bird no longer looked like a bird. It looked like a round mound of fluff and feathers. I screamed when I saw the deadness of the bird and threw a towel over the cage. Furiously, I called Hannah Lee. Oh, no! She was out of town! Had she warned me of her leaving? Had she jumped ship abandoning me? I called her backup psychologist. My head was jumbled, my body tense. I couldn't think straight and could not be in the same room as the bird cage. The backup psychologist evidently heard my distress for a few hours later Hannah Lee called from clear across the country to help me calm down. Her voice and manner were upbeat and brought me great relief. The bird had died. Not me. I could find someone else to dispose of the dead bird. First I calmed down. Then it hit me. Hannah Lee, Ms. Famous World Traveler, had called me from a city far away to help me calm down because my bird had died. Amazing. I couldn't believe it. A part of me began to trust her. Hannah Lee, Ms. Famous World Traveler, cared. About me. Amazing.

THE NEED FOR CONTAINMENT

Containment: What a powerful concept in therapy! When clients are so full of feeling that they are overwhelmed and unable to cope with the world, it is the therapist and the therapeutic space that assist in neutralizing the dangerous emotions the client is experiencing. Lili was able to utilize the office as a safe, familiar and soothing place that would contain some of her overwhelming feelings long before she was able to utilize me in this way. Gradually, however, she was able to allow me to contain some of the feelings that were overwhelming her.

One way of neutralizing dangerous emotions is by distinguishing between feelings and behaviors. The feelings are acceptable, but acting on the feelings is not acceptable. Another strategy is to use hypnosis to allow the client to visualize "putting the feelings away." A third strategy is to help the client process what she is feeling. This is similar to what a good parent does when a toddler is throwing a tantrum. Either physically or emotionally, the parent holds (contains) the child and names the feeling. Once the feeling is named, you can begin to teach the child how to cope. "I can see you are really angry. You may not hit me, but you can tell me why you are upset." This kind of mirroring teaches the client to become aware of, recognize, label, and accept her feelings. What she is feeling is internal and belongs to her. Recognizing this begins to build a boundary between what is me and not-me. In other words, it helps in the development of a sense of self.

Initially, because Lili did not have a sense of self, she was not always able to distinguish whether feelings were hers or someone else's. With no sense of agency, her own thoughts and feelings sometimes appeared foreign to her, as when The Gray and White One was angry or Vicky or Val were sad or hurt. On the other hand, she sometimes projected her feelings onto me. She would say, "You seem angry today." This was often a clue that she was angry AT me, but too frightened of her anger to claim it as her own.

Containment is a beautiful concept. The ability to contain denotes simply holding something for (or with) another until she is able to manage it on her own. It is a very different concept from swallowing something, which incorporates it and claims it as your own. A key therapeutic skill is being able to distinguish the client's feelings from those of the therapist. Being the "holder and caretaker" of Lili's pain meant taking it in, processing it, naming it, and giving it back in manageable pieces. Lili's fantasy of containment ("Hannah Lee and a baby me") suggests that the feelings that were too big for her to manage alone could be safely contained and managed by us together.

• •

"Tell me. What you are telling yourself?"

"I see an elephant in the clouds. That reminds me, I've got to get my piano tuned. Do you play an instrument? Why do you smile every time I look at you?"

"It's a natural reaction for me. I'm just a natural smiler, I guess."

Silence. Lili's foot began twitching and bouncing again. Then it began thumping the couch with its bounce. Harder and harder, faster and faster. Her face became a stone statue of intense feeling. More silence broken only by the sound of Lili's thumping foot.

"Tell me what your foot is saying."

Silence stretched itself out into seconds, then minutes. The minutes felt like hours. Finally, Lili spoke.

"You are going to kick me out. You won't let me stay. I want to hide behind the chair so you can't find me. You make me go home. I don't want to go."

"Yes, you will have to leave. We have about five minutes left. But, I will see you again next week."

Tears welled up in Lili's eyes. "I don't want to go," she cried. The tears poured. Lili curled up in a ball. Her mind raced with the agony of leaving. She didn't have to work at pretending in here. She didn't have to worry about acting "normal" in here. She could just be. Forty-five measly minutes a week just to be. It wasn't fair. Why couldn't she stay?

Although it often seemed we had accomplished nothing, I never wanted to leave a therapy session. Leaving meant I had to wait seven days before the next respite from life. Leaving meant I would not be near a calming presence for seven days. Leaving meant I had to go through that agonizing weekly detachment. Leaving meant I somehow had to come out of the fog. Leaving meant a part of me would be missing for the next 168 hours.

I had to work myself up to feeling capable of leaving. I moved not at all at first notice of our time being up. Then slowly I would move. Put on my shoes. Stand up. Put the couch back together. Straighten the pillows. Pick up my stuff. Slowly, painfully, work my way toward the door. Hannah Lee got to where she would just open the door and walk out leaving me alone to work my way out of her office. As I moved, the count down of the next 168 hours began. Sigh. On occasion, something special happened. Hannah Lee and I left for home at the same time. When we did, it slowed down and delayed the process of disconnecting. I was filled with importance and joy when we shared an elevator ride to the parking garage. The children in me felt special and chosen. Going down the elevator with Hannah Lee was like that special Sunday outing. I probably should have worn short white gloves and a fancy hat.

I wonder if Hannah Lee ever wanted to let me stay but didn't because of her always present boundaries. My private wish.

The Role of the Therapist

Lili entered my office the first time seeking what many clients want from therapy and from a therapist: to "make it all better". Unfortunately, that is beyond the capabilities of most of us! Instead, we have to work hard to resist the temptation to provide gratification and instead provide therapy—a much more difficult task!

It was Lili's goal to duplicate in the therapeutic relationship what she had come to expect in other relationships. Either I was to merge with her, seeing and doing things her way; or, she was to elicit enough information from me to allow her to merge with me. Neither of these ways of relating would be helpful. A necessary part of therapy was to establish clear enough boundaries to communicate my expectation that she was to be in control of herself and her life; and that I was to be in control of myself and my life. Over time, this contributed to Lili developing a more cohesive sense of self.

The roles of both the client and the therapist are complex and demanding. Lili believed that "sweet gentle love hadn't much of a chance" against her rage and fear, anger and depression. But love is not always sweet and gentle. Love, in the therapeutic sense, is understanding.[5] And love is caring enough to stand firm and refuse to capitulate when that is called for. Rage and fear, anger and depression, actually haven't much of a chance against truly caring.

It is the therapist's job to be in charge of therapy, even when the client wants to take over. It is the therapist's job to insist that the client be in charge of herself, even when she wants you to take that responsibility. Thus, therapy is always a balancing act.

It begins with the very important task of developing a therapeutic relationship. Such a relationship calls for unconditional positive regard[6] for the client as well as very clear behavioral boundaries. The most important boundary is one of safety. Harming self or others is absolutely not acceptable.

It is the therapist's job to understand the client—her thinking, her feelings, her behaviors—and to in turn help her understand herself. This encompasses evaluation and assessment leading to a diagnosis, but it includes much more than that. Understanding must be consistent and constant, and must lead to treatment interventions that are helpful to the client. As Lili described it, the therapist must be able to calm and soothe the client so she can find clarity of thought and courage to share. Developing trust in one another is a part of this process.

Lili was absolutely correct in stating "it often seemed we had accomplished nothing" at the end of a therapy session. If I had been required to write a report to a managed care company every six sessions or so, I would have been in a real bind. How do you justify sitting quietly with a client curled up in a ball on your couch watching elephants in the clouds? Yet Lili's experience of those sessions was that "leaving meant I had to wait seven days before the next respite from life." Lili's experience was that the containment of therapy saved her life.

• •

5   WATKINS, JOHN. (1978) THE THERAPEUTIC SELF. NEW YORK: HUMAN SCIENCES PRESS

6   ROGERS, CARL. (1961) ON BECOMING A PERSON. BOSTON: HOUGHTON MIFFLIN COMPANY

Twenty

I think in pictures. Yes, my thoughts are in words, too, but the pictures often dominate. People and events have their place in my head with these pictures. During the years of my mental illness, the pictures and words chased one another around in confusion. Trying to decode and decipher the whirling mass to discover what my head was telling me often seemed impossible.

When my head would reach a boiling point, I couldn't function effectively. It would take every ounce of whatever secret unknown there was within me to make it through the public exposure of everyday life. In therapy, an ambivalence of sorts would occur. Here, I was in that supposedly safe place and the stuff within me wouldn't come out with any ease, if at all. I might wrap myself around the pillows filled with tension, stiff as frozen meat. Often, my foot would go into action shaking like a wet dog. The office would fill with silence and tension on my side of the room, while Hannah Lee calmly, serenely (and always perky) waited. And waited. And waited. On occasion, my tension might lead to my talking. More often Hannah Lee would speak first. One of her favorite remarks focused on my frantic foot: "What is your foot saying?" Now I tell you, I might have had problems knowing what was real or not-real, but I knew feet couldn't talk. However, I usually answered, "I don't know." Then there might be another pause, this one shorter, and then some words might spill out of my mouth possibly leading to conversation. At times, my arm would start hitting my head. Hannah Lee was quick to tell me that hitting was not allowed and must stop. She would ask me, "What are you telling yourself?" Any time I would go somewhat crazy in reaction to life — whether real or not-real — Hannah Lee would ask that very question. Some erratic response to some perceived event would cause me to freak out, and Hannah Lee would once again ask, "What are you telling yourself?" My typical answer would be, "Nothing. It is just happening."

Then Hannah Lee would give her "listen to your body" speech asking what was happening within my body; what and where was I feeling something physically. Sometimes I would be able to tell her, other times I hadn't a clue. Occasionally, it might have been a stubbornness ruled by fear that stopped me from answering. If I answered her question, a discovery might be made. What if I were not ready for the discovery? What if the discovery led to more excruciating pain? I wasn't always ready for discovery.

Not only did I see my thoughts as pictures, my thought process was very tangential in nature. Being tangential was like walking several different paths around the pond simultaneously to get to the scum or pearl that was right in front of me. This was the only way I could do therapy for a very long time. On the surface, much of what I said had no relation to therapy. On the other hand, it had everything to do with therapy. My tangential conversation served as a path to get to a point where therapy was possible. Oddly enough, my tangential thought process helped me organize what I had to say and helped me develop the courage to delve into some therapeutic issue.

Thankfully, Ms. Hannah Lee learned how to engage in my tangential thinking. I was quite distracting bouncing around with words and thoughts and pictures. Hannah Lee would sometimes ask how things I said related to therapy. Sometimes she would just sit in silence waiting. Amazingly enough, less tangential stuff would start to happen in the final ten to fifteen minutes of the therapy session. The "stuff" was often intense or explosive in nature and Hannah Lee would say it had to wait until next time.

Hannah Lee believed I was in control of my thoughts and should bring issues up at the beginning of sessions. I knew better, of course; I knew I needed more time. I begged for double sessions. Hannah Lee said she didn't do double sessions. I begged for twice weekly sessions. Hannah Lee said, "Only in emergency."

My heart cried out, "Aren't *I* an emergency?!"

In my repeated requests to have longer sessions, Hannah Lee always said no. She probably thought I would just be tangential for a longer time and still not be therapeutic until the end of the session. I disagreed with this, of course, but never was I given an opportunity to find out. Darn those boundaries!

Fear pretty much ran my life. I feared people. I feared their smiles, their words, their touch. I yearned for their smiles, their words, their touch. I feared myself. I didn't know what was me. The whole issue of real not-real or "you + me = I" may be difficult to understand. What may be more difficult to understand is how "grounded" I was in this false reality. Hannah Lee would often point out logical realness that I couldn't agree with. For example, the people in my head. I truly believed there were a bunch of people living inside me. I believed they were distinct from me.

I could see them and hear them. I couldn't always understand these people because of all the noise they made. They didn't look like me or sound like me. Vicki did look a little like me when I was little, with her bangs and short dark hair, but I never equated her with being me or a part of me. Never. Her anger and outrage probably stopped me from accepting Vicki as being a part of me. Even now, while I know she was a part of me, it is difficult to accept.

Fear held me captive in the possibility of being discovered. Within this fear my body and mind swirled as if drowning. Wave upon wave of fear pressed against me. The fear would bind me up into thoughts that would not stop or actions that could be harmful. Within this world of fear, Hannah Lee told me I had a fantasy world. That set my brain into a frenzy. I was adamant that it was all real. Again, there was fear. For some reason, I equated "fantasy" with "crazy." So if I lived in a fantasy world then I must be crazy. The one thing I was certain of was that I didn't want to be identified as crazy. It is one thing to feel crazy. It is something else altogether to be labeled crazy. Hannah Lee attempted to assure me that I was not crazy. She would try to talk me through what I believed was crazy and compare it to what I believed about myself. She wasn't always successful, and the next time Hannah Lee brought up my fantasy world, there my head would go again—fantasizing.

Speaking of fantasizing …

Vicki attended a session with me once. Body memories were thrashing their way through my body. Blackness paraded across my vision letting glimpses of Vicki into my mind's eye. Within these visions and body memories, Vicki was expressing her fear of the man. "He's coming to get me," she cried. My body tightened and convulsed in fear, experiencing sensations and events that were only occurring in my mind. Hannah Lee had to do the hypnotic one to five, five to one count to help me "come to" and become able to drive home. Hannah Lee later told me she never saw Vicki, i.e. I never "became"

"He's coming to get me"
Vicki's appearance in
Hannah Lee's office 9/8/94.
This is how I saw her.

Vicki. It was only I who saw her.

There were things I needed to tell Hannah Lee, but I couldn't figure out how. One day a brilliant childlike plan came to me: tell Hannah Lee what I had to say using my Barbie™ dolls! I had always been fascinated with the idea of play therapy. Here was my chance to see it at work. I could tell that Hannah Lee wasn't overly enthusiastic about this brainstorm, but she didn't stop me. The whole session is a blur. In my head, I knew I had to do this. My hope was to share my story and in the story make discoveries about Val, Vicki and the dark man. I thought that if I "played" with my dolls, answers would come. The results were questionable. What I remember about this session is that I sat on the floor behind a chair. The chair was both the stage and my protection. I think the chair's wall of protection was almost more important than the "show." I remember getting out the dolls, and I remember feeling myself becoming younger and smaller. I remember picking up the dolls and moving them. What I don't remember is what the dolls did and said. The strongest sense of that session is of being little and confused. I don't know whether the confusion was that of the grown-up who walked into Hannah Lee's office or if it was the little girl sitting on the floor hiding behind the chair playing with dolls. What was the message I needed to convey? I do not know that either. I do remember feeling silly and stupid when it was all over. Although I remember so little of this event, the fact of its existence has always been important to me. This session also reminds me of one of Hannah Lee's most common statements: "Listen to your insides, ask yourself questions." Hannah Lee wanted me to get my answers from within myself. I was constantly begging her to tell me about myself, to answer questions about herself in hope of finding more about me. Yet, Hannah Lee insisted the answers about me were inside me. All I had to do was listen, as if listening to my inside self (selves?) was that simple. How does one listen to oneself? There were all those bits and pieces of people holding their own conversations inside my head. There were all those people holding conversations outside my head. I didn't know where to listen and when I did decipher what someone was saying, I was often uncertain in how what was said related to my me. It didn't help that I could not always differentiate internal from external, real from not-real. So what was I supposed to listen to and what was I supposed to internalize and make a part of me?

Of course, I was not completely out of touch with reality. In fact, I appeared very much in touch with the real world to people who knew me. How I did it I will never know—for that successful aspect of my life I give full credit to God. Still, my amazement continues that people could not see my craziness, especially since I was so convinced everyone could see inside me. How could I have this strange world that I experienced as real, yet have no one else see it? It just doesn't make sense. Or does it? I mean I was the one with the odd sense of reality. Everyone else was normal and not looking for the abnormal. They saw what they expected to see, and accepted any uniqueness as simply a part of me. I was the one lacking acceptance.

For the most part, therapy sessions left me with little memory of events or words said. If anything left a session with me, it wouldn't light up in my brain as a memory until later; sometimes the knowledge of memory didn't come to the forefront of my brain for more than a year. Therapy always made an impression, and sooner or later I would become cognizant of those impressions.

As therapy and years progressed I began sneaking peeks at Hannah Lee. Often, she would notice and smile. "Why do you keep smiling at me?" I would query in suspicious tones. She would say it was a natural response. In my wariness and lack of trust, I did not want Hannah Lee to notice that I was looking at her. I just wanted to sit and gaze at her, absorb her at my leisure without all the danger of eye contact. You know, her ability to see inside of me and discover all that rampant terribleness. Hannah Lee would insist that she could not see inside of me. I, as usual, knew otherwise.

Torment was mine when Hannah Lee refused to answer my questions of a personal nature. I needed to be able to see Hannah Lee in my head. With all the noise and words constantly shoving against one another, my gift for seeing and thinking in pictures was the only way I could organize my head. If I could see Hannah Lee in my head, a certain calmness existed for me outside her office. Her refusal to answer my rampage of questions became an internal fear that I would not be able to think of her in my one relatively calm mode of thinking—in pictures. I often told her that I needed a place to put her outside of therapy. Hannah Lee did not offer up any answers to give me my pictures. Boundaries, she called it. Meanness and misunderstanding I called it. Though useless, I continued my asking in hope, always in hope. Also, knowing Hannah Lee would most likely not answer my questions, I set myself up to maintain my anger with her. I feared letting my guard down with her. I didn't know whether I could truly trust her. What if she dumped me, too? Over the years, I learned to ask fewer and less intrusive questions, and Hannah Lee came to answer some. It was much better then.

Eventually, Hannah Lee and I developed a relatively good relationship. I began to appreciate her and even her boundaries. I didn't like her boundaries, but did come to appreciate them. And toward the end of our therapeutic relationship, I could even joke about boundaries, hers and mine.

On her part, Hannah Lee finally allowed bits and pieces of herself and her life to be shared. When she first became Ms. Famous World Traveler, she would tell me about one month in advance that she would be disappearing. Okay, she said she was traveling to somewhere outside the country. It was my perception that she disappeared. Hannah Lee always adamantly claimed she did not disappear. She also always promised to come back.

Change always threw me for a loop. I depended on the world around me being constant so I wouldn't become more confused than I already was. Hannah Lee was constantly making changes. New hairstyles. New hair colors. New cars. New name. And new office furniture. On and on it went. The changes felt relentless. The fog of my head just couldn't handle such unknowns.

When there was a change in furniture or offices, I would stand and stare at the room uncertain of my place within it. As Hannah Lee began with fervor working toward becoming Ms. Famous World Traveler, she allowed a psychiatrist to share her office. I hated him sight unseen. He was invading our private space. Little aggravating touches crept into our space. A little waterfall. A new desk. His credentials. The couch.

Oh, the couch! The doctor and Hannah Lee bought new furniture for the office of which one was a small couch, slightly too big to be considered a true love seat. Hannah Lee had failed to warn me about this enormous change in her office. I walked in and froze, staring, uncertain of my place in this new uncomfortable environment. Hannah Lee declared the room perfectly comfortable and stated that she liked it. I could sit wherever I wanted, she said. Well, the chairs looked scary and unsafe. I had always sat on the couch in the past so that was where I chose to sit. I decided that I fit well on that couch and could sit on it lengthwise and with the pillows to cover me, I could be safe. It was okay for a couple of weeks. Then that invader doctor decided to put a thick board under the cushions. Now, I am no princess able to feel a pea, but the millisecond I sat on that couch, I knew something was wrong. I leaped off that couch yelling about how hard it was. Screaming and throwing the cushions to the floor, I discovered the offending board. I yanked that heavy board off the couch, which was not easy, and railed at the injustice of having to share the office with such a person. Thus began a ritual for the remainder of time we used that office. Start the session by tearing the couch apart and repairing it to my satisfaction. End the session by returning the blasted board to the couch. At first, Hannah Lee would help me put the couch back together. After a time she just left me to it.

When I was about to study psychological testing at school, I made a couple of requests. I wanted to retake the Rorschach, that famous ink blot test, and I wanted to take an IQ test. The inkblots were as scary now as when I had taken this test during my second hospital stay. I saw all sorts of things I didn't want to see.

The IQ test was a lot more fun. It was like playing a bunch of games. My strength proved to be verbal skills, and my weakness was in social skills; i.e. reading social situations accurately. On the verbal portion of the test, there was one question I fell in love with. This question asked how two seemingly unlike objects were alike. I was so enamored with this question that I wrote page after page comparing the two objects. This kept me occupied for days. I could have written a short book filled with my comparisons. I would love to publish the book, but the IQ people would probably become angry with how I skewed their test. In reality, I doubt many people would have read the book. I mean, really now.

Regarding my poor reading of social situations, Hannah Lee said that was probably due to my developmental issues: wanting to be a child, wanting someone else to take care of me. We sometimes wondered if my amazingly rapid development in babyhood somehow aided in my missing other essential things in babyhood. Whatever the reason, I do know I often felt unfit or unworthy at social gatherings. People made me nervous. It took way too much energy to contain myself in the midst of a gathering. I was fearful, apprehensive, and suspicious. What did these people want from me? What were they expecting of me? What if someone talked to me? There was simply too much pressure at social gatherings. I was afraid to talk to people because something seemingly innocuous might set off the explosive noise in my head. It was very nerve-wracking.

Ego development

In these pages, Lili shares the gravity of her lack of ego development. When she began therapy, she had difficulty distinguishing real from not-real, internal from external, or self from other. She was confused about visions, body memories, and hallucinations. While in her mind's eye she could see and hear "people" in her head, there was no outward sign of their existence.

Lili desperately looked for definition of her self through merger with others. Her pressure for me to pray at the end of sessions was an expression of her symbiotic longing. Because previous therapists defined her as

MPD, she defined herself as MPD. She was convinced that they, and I, could see inside of her and that we should therefore be able to give her definition. If I could not or would not give her the answers she sought, then possibly she would find answers through her Barbie™ dolls. When even the Barbie™ dolls did not help Lili define her self, she continued to try to define her self by demanding information about me. When I refused those demands, she wanted to "absorb" me through her gaze. Possibly absorbing or swallowing me, internalizing me as a part of her, would allow her to feel complete. This is reflected in her equation that "you + me = I". Any answer would do except the one I continually presented her with: that the answers to who she was were within her, contained by her.

In addition to the deficits in her sense of self, Lili had a child's eye view of change. To Lili, if I *looked* different I *was* different. If my style of dress or my hair color changed, in Lili's mind I was no longer Hannah Lee. This lack of object constancy with me and with others resulted in a lack of trust and a tremendous fear of people. Lili was unable to make sense of people or to understand what they might want from her. This resulted in a great deal of fear, anxiety, and anger.

Given consistency and clear boundaries, Lili came to know over time that I would continue to be myself despite changes and transitions in my life. Along with developing object constancy, Lili developed trust in me and in herself. As trust increased, Lili's need to control me decreased. Developing more of a sense of her own boundaries, Lili became more clear about who she was separate from me. And, as Lili's boundaries developed, my own boundaries could be less rigid.

• •

Twenty-one

YEAR ONE: I have been diagnosed as having MPD, Multiple Personality Disorder. The diagnosis came about during a two and a half week stay at an inpatient psychiatric unit.

My point of view concerning this diagnosis cycles. One minute I come up with MPD jokes; next I am bawling in despair. Another moment I am writing a book in my head, and next I won't be believing myself or the diagnosis at all.

Disbelief in myself is strong, yet only with belief and trust can I be "cured". Part of the problem lies in the appearance or presentation of my personality system. To the best of my knowledge the alternate personalities (alters) never have total control. They are voices in my head or actions I do with me semi-cognizant of what goes on. I may not be able to stop myself from doing something, or my mind may perseverate on a thought

YEAR TWO: Hannah Lee does not believe I have MPD. She says she sees fragmentation and psychotic depression. So what is the correct diagnosis? Hannah Lee says she believes me more than anyone else has. She is not Dr. Claws who did not listen to a thing I said. She says I may or may not have MPD, but that she hasn't seen it. If I am not allowed to define myself as MPD, I have no definition.

YEAR THREE: I think I am more afraid of NOT "switching" personalities in the company of Hannah Lee than of "switching". I know that a while ago I chose to give my diagnosis up into the hands of God, but I fear I have grabbed it back. I wonder if I am trying to fit myself into the mold of MPD just to prove something to Hannah Lee. On the other hand, Val and Vicki do seem to exist. I do disappear here and there and have some lapses in memory. Those who made the MPD diagnosis stated that I was very high functioning and only mildly affected by the malady overall, but that it was rather obvious while I was there. You can't and don't diagnose that which you cannot see.

But, if this MPD malady is rather mild, why worry about it? What if I only appeared to be MPD and really am not? I don't know. The diagnosis proved to me that I am not crazy. I struggle with my diagnosis, and whether or not I am crazy, but cannot talk about it with Hannah Lee. I'm not sure I want to talk about it with Hannah Lee. I don't want her to be right because then she would have won all the wars. At the same time, if I don't stop worrying about the realities of the Multiple Personality Disorder diagnosis, will we ever get anywhere? I am afraid of falling apart in session because Hannah Lee will kick me out at five no matter what. She doesn't care if I am in little pieces. She just stands up, and it is over. I don't like Hannah Lee in this respect. I wonder how she feels about getting closer to fifty. She's still got a few years before then. Sometimes I want to quit therapy just so we can be friends. Sometimes I want to go to her church in hope of seeing her outside the office. She makes herself so untouchable in the office; I would like to see her somewhere else. Hannah Lee's always telling me I am trying to control her. I disagree. I would just like to win the occasional battle. She's always telling me it is my therapy, but then she infers I have to do it her way. How I wish we could just hold regular conversations.

Hannah Lee desires this event to be recorded: For once we stopped our therapy session on a note of relief rather than my anger.

Many people dislike labels, and I can see their point, especially when it comes to being crazy. However, the labels of mental illness brought me comfort rather than discomfort. A diagnosis brought relief.

As I already mentioned, Hannah Lee did not join the bandwagon of those who said I have Multiple Personality Disorder. She told me that she hadn't seen it, and until she did, she would question the diagnosis.

Accurate diagnosis took awhile. The long-term common thread was depression. That much Hannah Lee and I could agree upon. Now, although I came to agree that MPD was not the accurate diagnosis for my problems, with that diagnosis came the first time therapists and medical professionals had actually listened to what I was saying and heard me. There were moments when I suddenly "woke up" and could not tell you what had gone on before. I felt as if, and believed, other people lived in my body. I was hearing voices. Under hypnosis, a couple of so-called alters made an appearance. Multiple Personality

Disorder had become a soothing diagnosis for me. It meant I was not crazy. It explained my experiences in a logical manner. Being labeled MPD took away some of my fears of insanity. Finally, there was an explanation. It felt good.

Agreeing to Disagree

Lili often became angry that I would not accept her diagnosis of Multiple Personality Disorder. After repeatedly accusing me of not believing her, I responded, "I believe you more than anyone else has." By that I meant that I observed and listened to her very closely, neither adding to nor subtracting from what she was saying. The diagnostic elements required for an MPD diagnosis were simply not present. Lili was able to say "to the best of my knowledge the alters never have total control. They are voices in my head or actions I do with me semi-cognizant of what goes on." The voices and actions *could* have been part of a total picture of having alter personalities. However, the diagnosis of MPD demands that alters alternately take control of the person and that they have their own individual way of perceiving and relating to the world.[7] I had never seen the changes in appearance, mood and behavior that I would expect to see in MPD. In addition, Lili did not have the memory gaps that plague dissociative clients.

The issue of diagnosis gave me a platform from which to practice with Lili the idea that "I am me" and "you are you." Rather than get in a control battle and insist that Lili agree with my perspective, I simply began to say that she "may or may not" have MPD, but that I had not seen it. It was okay with me for her to have her own thoughts, ideas and perspective. I reserved that same right for myself. Although Lili admitted to being more afraid of NOT switching than switching because she wanted me to agree with her diagnosis, she was also able to admit "If I am not allowed to define myself as MPD, I have no definition." For Lili, the diagnosis did bring relief and was, in her words, "how I avoided my self." I, of course, was still left with the dilemma of what then *was* Lili's diagnosis.

Lili's previous experience in therapy had been that her emotions were a means of controlling others, particularly her therapist, rather than being useful as important signals to herself. Learning to tolerate her feelings depended on her being able to experience, express, and verbalize her feelings appropriately. Because her experience had been that feelings were too overwhelming to manage, she thought feeling meant falling

7   American Psychiatric Association (1994). Diagnostic and Statistical Manual of Mental Disorders, Fourth Edition. Washington, D.C.

apart. And, as she stated, "I am afraid of falling apart in session because Hannah Lee will kick me out at five no matter what." While this was a bit of an exaggerated fear, it was true that I insisted on having clear boundaries and that I wanted to communicate to Lili my confidence and expectation that she was capable of learning to manage her feelings without being overwhelmed by them.

• •

The problem with the MPD label was that while it was soothing, it was inaccurate. While I would "fog out" and be unaware or act differently from usual, there really were no alters. No different personality came out and interacted with other people as a separate person. My head heard voices, and sometimes the words of these voices would come out through my mouth. I believed these people in my head had control over themselves and me. I did dissociate; that was how I survived the pain and fear of that raging anger and the perceived abuse. It was how I avoided my self.

However, the MPD label was not accurate.

When Hannah Lee gave me the famous inkblot test, interesting data came up pointing in the direction of psychosis rather than MPD. I was not schizophrenic, praise the Lord, and Hannah Lee agreed. Between the inkblot results, my not being able to sleep, having people talking in my head all the time, the body memories of molestation, and, of course, the depression, a new and final diagnosis came about: Schizoaffective Disorder. This was scarier than some diagnoses, but had better hope than other diagnoses. This diagnosis angered and scared me. Maybe I was nuts. How close to Schizophrenia was Schizoaffective Disorder? I was adamant about not being Schizophrenic, and had to agree that I did fit the criteria for Schizoaffective Disorder.

Schizoaffective Disorder Depressive Type consists of some of the characteristic symptoms of Schizophrenia[8] such as hallucinations, disorganized speech or flat affect[9] (all were my symptoms) alongside major depressive episodes. Part of the time the characteristic symptoms appear alone, without the depression. Part of the time they are present with the depression. These disturbances cannot be due to effects of drug abuse, medication or a general medical condition.

Add in the depression and some dissociation and whooey; shouldn't I be

---

[8] Information gathered from DSM IV: American Psychiatric Association. Diagnostic and Statistical Manual of Mental Disorders, Fourth Edition. (1994) Washington, D.C. (This manual was in effect when I was diagnosed.)

[9] Monotone, neither happy nor sad, a lack of showing emotion

living in the loony bin?

Positive things would eventually come out of this final diagnosis. For one thing, Hannah Lee and I finally agreed about something.

With the diagnosis came a new psychiatrist, Dr. Bestwell. Dr. Bestwell is one worthy doctor. He listens and hears what I am saying. He asks questions that draw out useful information. He doesn't appear to form an opinion before he gets the data in person.

While each doctor and therapist was important in my move toward being more "normal" and sane, Dr. Bestwell and Hannah Lee were the two most responsible for the positive growth of my mental wellness and the diminishing of my symptoms. I do have to thank Harry for knowing when to refer me.

Dr. Bestwell's contribution to my wellness included not only his listening skills, but finding the right meds. I hated medicine. I wouldn't even take aspirin for a headache. Going a bit crazy seems to have had a part in changing all that. When I was first hospitalized, Dr. Claws decided that I was histrionic, i.e., overly emotional and attention seeking. He put me on some drug that had no effect. Nope. There were no side effects and no other effects either. Dr. Claws didn't seem to notice that no improvement occurred with this medication. A couple of years later, Dr. Forest put me on something else. It didn't do anything for me either. Still, I was a good little girl and took whatever they said I should take. In my state of depression and suicidal thoughts, I was also lost and often felt outside of myself. People told me to take medications, I did. Since I kept swirling on that downward spiral, I would say nothing had done the trick.

I had been going seriously crazy for about two and a half years before any medication success came. First, Dr. Keyes at the second hospital had prescribed an antidepressant that did some good. I was taken off the other medication(s) I was on at the time. When I began meeting with Dr. Bestwell, he upped the dosage of the antidepressant. This lightened my load a bit. However, the antidepressant was not the total answer. With the new diagnosis of Schizoaffective Disorder a few years later, and with the listening skills of Dr. Bestwell, a newly developed anti-psychotic was prescribed to be taken along with the antidepressant. The difference was amazing. It didn't happen all at once, but the noise and voices in my head began to diminish. I was able to sleep at night. I was able to think almost clearly, something that hadn't been possible for years. Although there was progress, it took several years for me to be able to see myself as being healthier. Without the medication prescribed by Dr. Bestwell, I don't think I would have gotten better. I may never have come to the calmness I now enjoy.

Controversy abounds with the use of medication. I questioned its use myself.

How could I be sure that it would be me handling my emotions and not the drugs? I feared the drugs would control me. I wanted to know that I would be in control, not the drugs. Yet, medication is what allowed the turnaround in my mental health status. My thought process and tightly active body loosened up a bit. Therapy could now take place. The sunrise was becoming visible on that distant horizon. It turned out that the drugs would control the chemical balance of my brain, and I would eventually control me. What a concept. What a relief.

And yet, I wasn't out of the woods. Not by a long shot.

SCHIZOAFFECTIVE DISORDER

An ongoing theme diagnostically for Lili was experiencing major depressive episodes consisting of depressed mood, lack of energy, feelings of worthlessness, an inability to concentrate, and thoughts of suicide or death.[10] She reported sometimes hearing voices and occasionally during sessions, her arm would suddenly commence hitting her head. While she reported having no sense of control over the bizarre behavior (avolition), she was able to stop herself when I firmly commanded that behaviors hurting herself or others were not acceptable. Tangential thinking (disorganized speech), short concrete responses (alogia; a lack of verbal spontaneity and poverty of speech), and a noticeable lack of feelings (flattened affect) were common during Lili's treatment. Combined with the depression, these symptoms led me to consider the diagnosis of Schizoaffective Disorder.[11] We discussed the diagnosis during our work together, and after years of agreeing to disagree, we finally had a diagnosis on which we could agree. This diagnosis explained Lili's disorganized behavior at work and her lack of a sense of agency.

About this same time, Lili found a new psychiatrist. Consistent with the diagnosis of Schizoaffective Disorder, he prescribed an antidepressant and an anti-psychotic medication. These were very effective in decreasing the physiological component of the overwhelming emotions Lili had been experiencing and in allowing her to feel much more stable and to make better use of therapy. I was amused and mildly indignant when Lili praised her new psychiatrist by saying, "He doesn't appear to form an opinion before he gets the data in person."

• •

10   AMERICAN PSYCHIATRIC ASSOCIATION (1994)

11   AMERICAN PSYCHIATRIC ASSOCIATION (1994)

Twenty-two

For the next few years, my jumbled state-of-being maintained a certain *status quo*. I guess the progress during this time was in developing a useful relationship with Hannah Lee and in my not getting worse. I definitely wasn't much better, just less of an emergency. This so-called maintenance eventually wore away. The noise in my head once again grew in volume. The voices would not shut up. They were so noisy that my job began to interfere with my world of confusion. It got so I could not tell the difference between the noise in my head and the noise of my first and second grade students. Perhaps I should use the words "voices" and "words," but it was all so indistinguishable that everything was just noise. I was almost back to having my head filled with that cacophony of screeching monkeys. For several months the noise increased. Again, there was no differentiating between real and not-real.

I have been having nightmares the last several nights. Not the kind that make you wake up screaming, but ones that are so disturbing that I wake up more worn out and tired than I was when I went to bed. For the most part, I cannot say what the nightmares are about. In fact, except for last night's nightmare, I do not remember anything about them. Here, I will attempt to tell the story of last night's.

I hear screaming. I run and run in a rural area to discover this woman lying on the ground with one of her legs severed. The ends of both parts of her leg look bloody and as if someone had tried to stop the bleeding by stuffing straw or hay into her legs. As I approach, she moans and screams to call 911. There is a service station or farm office across from where she is lying. I run toward the building to call 911. A strange looking man with bleeding scars on his face runs toward this woman as I race to the phone. The woman is his mother. I can sense that he doesn't want me to call 911, but I go into the building and call anyway. When I give directions to get to the farm, I tell them that we are five miles south of the town. The problem is we are north of the town. I go out to the woman and the man. He is angry with me. She is dead, which is what he wanted. Then I realize that the ambulance is not there because I gave 911 the wrong directions. I go in and call them again. This time when I go into the farm office it is a car repair shop. There is a boy in a wheelchair. He is missing most of his limbs. He takes a bent exhaust pipe and puts it on his arm stub and uses it as his arm. I think the ambulance comes and picks up the dead woman. The man is really mad at me now because his mother's body is taken away. He wanted to keep her. Then the scene switches, or rather, the characters change. Now there is a mother, the man's wife. She has three little girls. One of the little girls has no legs. They are all young children. The girl with no legs cannot get down the stairs so she usually slides down the vent. One day, the three girls climb to the uppermost reaches of the house. The mother calls to the girls. They realize that they cannot get down. But, it is really the oldest girl, the one with no legs, who cannot get down. The mother tells her to drop down the fireplace flue. She does as her mother tells her. The other two girls decide to follow her rather than go down the stairs. Nobody is there to catch the girls and with three of them falling there is more force. All three girls die as they crash upon one another at the bottom of the flue. Then the mother dies. I don't know how she died. The man becomes very upset and hateful toward me. I am not sure how, I just don't remember, but I lose my head (literally) and am still alive. The man, it turns out, is made of artificial body parts. He wants his wife back. He decides to take her head and put it on my body so he can have his wife back. I have no head, yet I can still think and see. The man takes his wife's body and opens her mouth to start taking off her face. I see him put an instrument into her mouth, and I close my eyes so I don't have to watch him do that awful cutting. I know her head ends up on my body, at least I think it does. I don't remember anything else.

GRIEF AND LOSS

Things were looking up. Lili and I agreed on a diagnosis. She had found a psychiatrist who listened to her and was able to prescribe medication that was helpful for her. Therapeutic relationships were finally forming that might make treatment not only possible but successful. Then life happened. Lili's grandmother, who lived in an adjoining town and provided some degree of safety and nurturance for Lili, was terminally ill.

Lili's nightmare gave me some insight into her worsening condition. I conceptualized the woman with the severed leg to be Lili's beloved grandmother who, in reality, had a terminal illness and was dying. Since the woman was the mother of the "strange looking man," the man was obviously Lili's father. The dream expresses Lili's ambivalence about her grandmother's death. Rationally, she is able to talk about it being better for her grandmother if she could die and not have to suffer. But emotionally, Lili, like the man in the dream, "wanted to keep her." The man's wife in the dream represents Lili's mom, who indeed had three little girls. Lili was the oldest, the little girl with no legs. The dream expresses Lili's feelings of confusion and helplessness at the loss of her grandmother. It also expresses Lili's feeling of confusion about who she is. Am I me, or am I my mother?

• •

I came home very despondent today. My job review was better, but I am told that I still have a very long way to go. Molly, my principal, said she would not allow me to teach in a regular classroom next year unless a major amount of improvement occurs.

I came home so upset that I went straight to bed. It was five o'clock in the afternoon. I put in a movie and slept through it. I called Hannah Lee and told her that if she wanted to know why I was in bed to call me. She evidently didn't care to know. She didn't call. I wanted her to call. I wanted her to soothe me. Or just to know. I guess that is it for tonight. THE END.

Three months later:

I want Hannah Lee here. I want to drown myself. I am very sad. I am tired of being horrible at this job of mine. I wanted to hurt somebody today. I mean I wanted to sling someone, anyone, across the room. I wanted to kick and hit and smash things up. I am so very tired of even trying to do things right. Today, one of the remediation team came and observed me in my classroom. She then attempted to "organize" my room. It was horrible. I began to disappear. It was so scary. I was overwhelmed. Everything began to swirl inside of me. I think all the voices began. I know I kept sinking inside of myself. It was very frightening. I kept thinking/saying/praying, "This can't happen now. I can't go away right now. Oh, God, I am slipping away." I remember that much. I could hear Julie's voice (the remediation mentor), but I couldn't understand her words. I could see her in the sense that there was shape and color, but she was not in focus. I just knew that the end was near. Then suddenly, I was almost back. I had to clench my fists and force myself to breathe. I couldn't look at Julie or what she was doing. I couldn't let myself hear her words. She just kept doing things with my stuff. I was hanging on to being by the fleeting strand of a spider web. Strong, but oh so vulnerable. I need help. What if it ever happens again? Would I ever really hurt somebody? What if my insides take over when I am with the children? I only fear if someone inside takes over. I need Hannah Lee, and she is out of town. She claims she will come back. She will. I hope. I pray. I just never trust her return until she is actually back.

LONGING FOR MERGER

Lili describes how out of control she feels during this period of time. She says, "I want Hannah Lee here. I want to drown myself." Psychoanalytically speaking, water symbolizes mother. My interpretation? The merger that Lili longs for is that described by Melanie Klein as "wanting to be inside of someone who is inside of you."[12] She is wishing for the safety and security of becoming part of the idealized object. She describes herself as "hanging on to being by the fleeting strand of a spider web," and she states "I only fear if someone inside takes over." It seems as though she wished that there *was* someone inside strong enough to take over.

Lili is describing here an important part of the therapeutic process. The therapist's role is sometimes to lend the client ego strength—"the strand of a spider web"—that allows her to hang on. The therapist provides a maternal function in supporting and encouraging the client's regulation and expression of affect. While the short-term goal is for the client to be able to use the ego support offered by the therapist, the long-term goal is for her to internalize that sense of safety and security for herself.

12   RALPH FISCH, PH.D., QUOTING MELANIE KLEIN, PERSONAL COMMUNICATION, DENVER, COLORADO, JUNE, 1994

Twenty-three

The more stress there was in my life, the more the people inside me would talk and make noise. The more voices and people inside of me, the more stress built up and affected my ability to function in the real world. Now the voices-stress cycle had begun its greatest escalation.

Grandma M. showed me the strength of love. During the year I lived with her, our time was filled with honest laughter and fun. We didn't ever hold deep discussions on anything, but with Grandma M. I felt completely and totally accepted. The time I lived with Grandma M. was one of my lighter years in the depression game. Something about Grandma's house brought a bit of peace to me. I loved that house with its creaky wooden floors and humungous, inviting kitchen. The house represented a haven, a place where the world couldn't get to me, and my terribleness was not visible. I loved Grandma M. I loved her house. One of my more persistent dreams was to own grandma's house and live there.

A little less than a decade after my year with Grandma M., when my world had collapsed and the darkness of my brain had taken over, things with Grandma changed. She became forgetful and unclean. She was unable to hold a conversation or follow along with what was going on around her. Grandma M. had developed Alzheimer's. One day, her hip broke and she fell. At this point, it was clear that Grandma M. could no longer take care of herself. Along with her broken hip, Grandma's Alzheimer's seemed to worsen at a daily rate and she was placed in a nursing home. I would go spend the night in Grandma's house and visit her at the nursing home on weekends. I would sing to her and hold her hand and share a meal. These were bittersweet times.

Then the floor was pulled out from under me. Grandma's house was to be sold. I freaked out. That house contained all the love a person could hold. I could stand in the center of the house and breathe in the love and gentle

142 ~ Kelly Ann Compton

spirit that permeated it. Now, that wonderful oasis was being sold, stolen from me. It had never occurred to me that I would lose Grandma's house before I lost Grandma, so the news that the house would be emptied and sold with Grandma less than a mile away devastated me. I was back to crying much of the time. The noise in my head increased. The people in my head swirled around each other in panic mode. It was a very difficult time.

I begged that nothing be done to the house until I could take pictures. I am now the proud owner of a five-inch stack of pictures of Grandma M.'s house! Someday, I will sort them and toss some. For now I have that five-inch stack. At the time, I needed those pictures for my safe haven was being taken from me. I always felt safe there with Grandma. I fervently wanted to be the one to buy Grandma's house, but it was out of my league. After taking the pictures, I volunteered to clean out and paint the kitchen. Even knowing that the house might be torn down or remodeled, I scrubbed every corner of that kitchen and painted the insides of the cabinets. It was a gift of love for Grandma and a way for me to say goodbye. I still have dreams about being in that house. Sometimes I can't tell what are memories and what are dreams.

While I made no claims at being a gifted teacher, I had my good points. I was often able to be with a child where he or she was at and could find a way to hook that child into academic growth. I could have ten kids in the room each doing his or her own thing and stay on top of it all. My weaker area was in discipline. I could seldom bring myself to follow through with disciplinary actions. I could see the strengths and fragile bits of my students and feared squashing them. Probably remnants from childhood. Now, with the stress-voice cycle escalating, my ability to teach was not looking good.

Things began to fall apart at work. I couldn't focus. I lost the ability to maintain *any* order in the classroom. I kept fogging out and could not maintain a presence with the children. My boss, Molly, noticed. The mayhem and noise in my class weren't hard to miss. Due to my seeming inability to take hold of a classroom and teach, I was put on special probation. I was observed, and I was sent to observe other classrooms. Three mentors, whose job it was to build up my ability to run a proper classroom, were assigned to me. Of course, no improvement occurred because my ineptness in the classroom came about because of my mental health state and not an inability to teach. This was a first, for until now I had been a decent teacher and my mental health issues had not injured my abilities to be safe and good regarding the children.

Hannah Lee began planting her feet firmly on the floor, sitting forward in her chair and speaking to me with grave concern. She spoke about possible legal and job-related issues. She worried about my ability to look out for myself. Hannah Lee advised me to seek legal counsel. She encouraged me to join the teachers' union. Hannah Lee was helping me to look out for myself. I think Hannah Lee was most concerned about what I shared with my coworkers and my boss. Boundaries of a concrete nature were needed in this situation, and I didn't have them. She even swore when I admitted to telling people I couldn't tell the difference between the voices in my head and the voices outside my head. Now, I can see her point. At the time, such confusion seemed so normal to me that I didn't think of other people and what they would think or how they would react. You don't stop yourself from what seems ordinary. One of the secretaries thought my comments to be the funniest thing she had heard in a long time. Every time I walked into the office she would get the giggles and tell me she remembered what I had said and that it cracked her up. I just laughed along with her. It was kind of funny. Her laughter, that is.

Finally, I had to admit that I could not perform my duties as a teacher. Hannah Lee was concerned, my boss was concerned, and I was too worn out from the noise to even freak out.

One fine morning, I was called into my boss's office for a discussion. One of the head honchos over Molly rattled off some story about himself once being a square peg in a round hole and how that could also be applied to me. He was, in effect telling me I should find a new job. My boss, Molly, on the other hand, was extremely supportive. She fought for me, and because of her, I was not fired.

I hate myself. I am a failure. I have not done good enough work at graduate school to be nominated for any awards. I allowed myself to get Bs when I was quite capable of doing A work. I gave into thinking Bs are all right. (Thank you Harry for that balderdash idea.) I just don't know enough and will not learn enough by March 25 to pass the graduate comprehensive exams. I am a failure. I am simply not good enough. Why can't I ever do good enough to receive an accolade? Why must I fail at everything I do?

I can't teach. I am a failure there too. I am no good. Those little children are suffering in their learning because of me. If I were good enough, they would be learning. I just hate myself. I am horrible. That is all there is to it.

I want to die. I want to write. I want to prove that I am worthy.

In my heart, I know I am not. Life sucks. I suck. I am one goddamn f*****g shit piece.

I should never have called my principal, even though she asked me to call, and I had been thinking of calling her. The combination of talking to her one night and then turning in my request for Restoration of Health Leave the next morning was just too much for me. It proved how horrible and inadequate I am. That is when I quit taking my medicine regularly. Why bother? It wasn't helping. I am not okay enough to hold down my job. I am a failure and a shit piece of personhood. I am not even a person. I don't deserve to be one.

I was losing weight and feeling proud of myself for losing twenty pounds in two years. I could wear a smaller dress size part of the time. I was working toward being a normal size person within ten years. It was working. I would be down to a normal size before diabetes got to me. But, no, that wasn't good enough. Diabetes decided to take over my body and destroy my plans. It was quite disgusting. I do what is right and the wrong attacks me anyway. I hate my body. I hate myself. I am no good. I am disgusting. Even what I do right is not good enough or fast enough. Nope. I am a failure. So I am eating all the sugar and fat that I can. And beef. Why eat healthy? It doesn't do any good anyway. I am trying to kill my heart. Passive long-term suicide. No one will know. They will think it was my weight. They will not know it was on purpose.

I am scared to death of being on half salary. I am missing one roommate. School expenses will be twice what I thought they would be because I forgot about the $1050 tuition for my internship. I haven't gotten my W-2 from last summer yet, so I cannot do my taxes. My tax return is crucial to my being able to survive on half salary. I haven't heard from the insurance company yet. My return on that is crucial also.

To put it bluntly, I hate myself and may not live much longer. I don't feel like it. I am a failure anyway, so why bother.

The end.

OVERWHELMED!

The stress in Lili's life became unbearable during her grandmother's illness. From her perspective, "my safe haven was being taken away." Concretely, her grandmother's house, which "contained all the love a person could hold," was being sold. Lili had not yet been able to internalize the feelings of love, safety and security that her grandmother's house represented to her. Once again, she was overwhelmed by feelings she couldn't manage.

Normally, grief and loss are resolved through mourning. However, the emotional deficits that Lili was dealing with made the development of the ability to mourn impossible. The result of this inability to mourn is depression,[13] and indeed Lili's depression deepened. The intense feelings she was unable to verbalize interfered more and more with her ability to think and organize. Historically, Lili had been a capable special education teacher. As her mental health worsened and her depression increased, this changed dramatically. She was put on probation and was in jeopardy of losing her job. She was experiencing far too much stress to be able to cope successfully. At this point, I encouraged her to seek a leave of absence from the school district where she worked.

The depression Lili was experiencing is obvious as she writes about her negativity toward herself. Her thoughts turn toward death, and she is so hopeless that things could improve that she discontinues taking her medication. It was at this low point that she was diagnosed with diabetes. Her depression was exacerbated both by her grandmother's illness and her own.

· ·

In the end, I did take a year of medical leave from my job. With words of wisdom from Hannah Lee, I managed not to spill my emotional guts to Molly or anyone else at work. No one knew why I was gone, and no one, not even Molly, knew how desperate my mental illness was.

When I went in to request medical leave, Molly was thankfully on my side. She believed in me and my future return to health when I had no such hope. Molly reassured me that depression was simply an illness and that it needed to be taken care of in whatever manner was necessary. Molly worked hard at helping me not to be fired. She saved my job for me while I was on leave. Molly definitely earned my respect and allegiance. I also give Molly credit for the quietness with which she handled my leave. Coworkers only knew I was not there. They did not know why.

Aah, the relief! At first, I just stayed home and sat, paced, or slept. This being my last year studying counseling in graduate school, I savored the luxury of only going to classes. Without the stress of attempting to contain myself at work, containing myself at graduate school was a bit easier. I even

---

13   KRYSTAL, HENRY. (1988). INTEGRATION AND SELF-HEALING. HILLSDALE, NEW JERSEY: THE ANALYTIC PRESS.

managed to write an independent study paper on self. Imagine me, the self-less one, writing a paper on self. Here is one brilliant quote: "Self. We strive toward being a self and defining whom or what that self is. As history moves along becoming a new and different present, the concept of self changes." My intellect must have taken over on this paper. It was definitely written before I knew my own self; that was to be a few years away.

During my counseling internship I discovered that I loved working with children under the age of ten, especially the five- and six-year olds. Their pain astonished me, but I found I could sit with them in their pain. I loved the freedom in being a counselor. Oh, there were rules to follow and techniques to use, but compared to teaching, I felt so free and capable. I had discovered in teaching that I was more interested in the emotional blocks behind the children's difficulties than their actual academic needs. I loved being a counselor. I was beginning to find my self while helping others find themselves.

Medical leave turned out to be filled with gifts. Just being allowed now to have a modicum of relaxation was extremely therapeutic.

Time now existed in which I could focus on myself without feeling guilty about it. I discovered that I liked the freedom of time to myself. Oh, how we become enmeshed with our work life. I discovered that my teaching had consumed precious moments of time where I should have, could have, been discovering my me and dealing with all that internal nightmare of crap. I no longer had to fight myself to maintain a front. What relief. I remember wandering the house in a fog of relief and disbelief. There was freedom—oh, the freedom!

Someday soon,
when I am young,
I shall do all the things
I've a yearning for.

It shall be grand
Just flitting around
or sitting still
For whatever I want
where ever I go

to be free for awhile
free to be me
alone for awhile
alone to find me.

Yes, medical leave offered the gift of freedom. Grandma M. was doing poorly now, and my new freedom allowed me to visit her more frequently.

I enjoyed the lack of predetermined structure in my days, yet I found a semblance of necessary structure, my own personal structure, to follow day by day. My sense of time was distorted; the day needed to have an order to it for me to get to places I needed to be. My pill box kept me aware of the right day of the week as long as I remembered to take my medications. The television gave me a sense of the time passing during the day. Regis? Better make certain I had eaten breakfast. Leeza meant lunch should be eaten soon. With Oprah, I knew I had best start fixing supper. I didn't really watch TV, I just left it on most of the time to give my day a sense of order. Though the lack of a minute by minute schedule was pure relief, the sense of order TV gave to my day was of vital importance. It helped keep me moving forward each day rather than stagnating in any particular pond of depressed psychosis.

At first, being home all day was eerie. I didn't know what to do with myself. I had never had such freedom of what to do and when to do it. Freedom required adjustment. Now there was time for all my confusion to reign freely. Initially, I would either stay in my bed hidden from the world or wander my house aimlessly. A sense of being lost permeated my inner being and lifted to the surface. Now there were fewer people or activities bombarding me with ordinary yet overwhelming expectations. The immediate relief felt powerful. My soul thirsted for the peace and calmness that might now be mine. Ah, time. There was now time to actually study for my classes. There was also time to actually read the required texts and proofread my papers. I became better able to converse with my fellow students, though conversational interchanges were kept brief and non threatening in nature, nothing too personal. Time abounded for such brain calming activities as prayer, sleep, or word puzzles. Sewing focused my brain off myself and off my confusion. Off the noise and voices in my head. I made quilts. I had time now to be a bit creative in the more normal fashion—drawing, writing, that sort of thing. I truly began to enjoy the therapeutic rhythm of this new life of mine, and in this rhythm some of my confusion began to dissipate. The noise within me lessened allowing me to differentiate between internal and external voices. My ability to focus on life without fear increased. Good things began to come from within me. I think this is where the therapy that would last truly began. I became more able to pay attention during therapy, to give attention to myself, and to give my attention to Hannah Lee. When Hannah Lee made suggestions or observations, I could almost hear and comprehend them.

Being on leave gave me a feeling of being in a delightful fluffy cloud of fog that could hide the cliff of despair from view. This sounds quite beautiful and serene. What it was was major pressure lifted from my façade of wellness. The number of hours a façade was required became minimal. Such relief.

Hannah Lee often told me to make choices or redirect my thoughts. Though I claimed and believed I couldn't stop my thoughts, I evidently did have that capability to a certain extent. At least enough to "look" normal. Perhaps I was able to pretend and use my imagination for that normal look. I don't know. What I do know is that whatever skill I had had at appearing to be a regular not crazy person stopped working. Hence, the medical leave.

Twenty-four

Strange things happened during this time. For instance, I was raped daily. Voices told me I had to sleep without panties on to be ready for the nightly rapes. During the day, all light disappeared when the rape began. My body could feel it. My mouth could taste it. I was unable to function when the body memories took over. Hannah Lee would tell me to open my eyes and look for the dark man. My eyes could never find him. My mind could never lose him.

The mind is a powerful thing.

Another strange thing that occurred was my having bowel movements in my panties and not knowing it until after the fact. I could be anywhere at any time, and it would happen. A lot of underwear got thrown away in store restrooms. I even discovered panties laying about my home covered with dried feces. Hannah Lee told me to listen to my body. How could you listen for something you didn't even know was happening? I certainly didn't know.

Hannah Lee and I had many debates. She would tell me to do something, I would say I didn't know how. Generally, Hannah Lee was attempting to ground me within the real world. I pretty much avoided it.

I don't know how to explain it. A part of me knew things weren't right. My world was one of confusion. All those people were swirling about inside my head with such a sense of actuality and realness that I couldn't be swayed to believe that they were simply parts of me. Their voices were unique and unlike mine. They were of different ages. The ones I could see had their own looks. And everybody had a name. I didn't name them—they told me their names.

It is awkward to be both sane and crazy at the same time. I knew that what I was living was not normal for the majority of people, but I also knew that all the people and pictures, and goings on inside of me were real. It was hard to believe life should be experienced differently.

Strange, too, was my inability to tell where I ended and another person began. How confusing! It was sort of like being a chameleon changing color with the scenery. As I entered the presence of another person, I would latch onto their "color." This was all very unconscious on my part. Perhaps as a chameleon finds safety in becoming the color of his surroundings. I, too, found a level of safeness. Not being able to distinguish myself as being separate spared me from that horribleness that was surely me.

Funny, isn't it. I feared people, yet unconsciously aligned myself with them, like that chameleon changing colors to camouflage itself. In therapy this translated itself into some of the questions I would pepper Hannah Lee with. "What did you think of …?" "Have you seen …?" "What do you believe about …?" I tried to discover what her faith in God was about in order to reassure myself about mine. I tried to find myself inside another person.

Often, I sensed that I was being stared at and I would react with a swift jerk of my head. Of course, no one was ever staring at me. Except Hannah Lee. On my sneak-a-peek-at-Hannah Lee looks, I would often find Hannah Lee staring at me. This caused distress. "Why are you staring at me?" I would spit out. "I'm not staring. People look at one another when they talk. I am just waiting." Then I would keep sneaking peeks to see if she were still staring. Every time our eyes met, Hannah Lee would smile a supposedly encouraging smile. Oh, did that irk me. And scare me.

I couldn't afford for Hannah Lee to like me because then I would have to like her and then trust her. The problem was, I had no trust in me so how could I trust Hannah Lee with me?

The act of trusting was a bit lopsided with me. On the one hand, I trusted no one. Fear and anger did not allow trust. My fear knew everyone was lying to me, or waiting to tear me apart. Anger knew they were out to hurt me. People were the visibly perceived enemy. On the other hand, I believed and accepted every word that came out of people's mouths. It was my innocence, my hopes, my dreams, that trusted and yearned for relationship. I searched for a reason to believe my hopes and dreams for relationship. I needed to believe in people and their goodness. Trust was simply a confusing issue for me.

Twenty-five

Besides needing to see pictures of things in my head in order to understand and accept them, I also saw the world in different ways at different times. Sometimes, when I stood up, the physical world appeared to me as small and distant and I felt like a physical giant. If I was walking as a giant, I needed to step carefully to make sure I found the floor. At other times, I seemed to be very little and the world seemed too big for me. Everything around me appeared to be larger than life and sometimes unreachable. My hands were not always the same size. They have seemed both long and slender and short and fat.

For a time I believed I was changing sizes. It was disconcerting to never know what size the world or I would be the next time I looked. I was surprised to discover that most people do not experience this as I do.

The only explanation I have for these odd perceptions of myself is that I felt myself to be changing ages constantly. One hour I would be a young child sucking my thumb and viewing the world through fearful eyes. The next I might feel several years older viewing the world with suspicion. The age I seldom felt was adult. I have wondered, when I stand up and everything appears small, if perhaps I am noticing that I am an adult. I never knew from day to day how I would experience the world around me; how I would experience myself. This made it difficult to relate to the world and the people within it. It also made finding my own self rather difficult. Who was I? How old was I?

Instances of changing my self-perception used to be something that I had to hide. Now, the experiences do not happen as often. I've no need to hide them either. Still, I don't go around asking people if the world has shrunk. I mean, I have learned something about boundaries! These days I am mostly just me. The world usually doesn't change size anymore. I don't know when that began to change. I only know that I don't worry as much about how I am like or unlike other people.

My perceptions of my physical body changed, too. Even when I was not experiencing myself to be changing sizes, I had no real knowledge of my size. I would sometimes view myself as fat, sometimes slender. Even now, I forget my size at times. Whenever I would look into the mirror, it would be with disbelief. Is that my body? The mirror always surprised me. Always.

Often, when looking into a mirror, I would not recognize myself. The face wasn't right. The hair wasn't right. I wasn't wearing my whipped cream dress. Logic would say it was me in the mirror. I mean, my body was supposedly the one standing in front of the mirror. *But where is my body?* I would think. The picture my head had of how I was supposed to look stopped at age nine. There is a picture of me in my photo albums at age nine. When I see that picture, I see me, the real me; the last time I remember that I felt to be me.

Worsening Symptoms

During this period of time, Lili was quite seriously ill. The intensity of her feelings of loss was traumatic and overpowering for her. Lili had several automatic and unconscious defenses against these unbearable feelings of sadness and anger. Rather than experiencing her feelings as internal and belonging to her, she projected them. She also experienced dissociation: modifications of consciousness that kept her feelings out of her conscious awareness. While this kept Lili from psychologically falling into a terrifying and traumatic black hole, it also resulted in her disturbed sense of time and in her changing perceptions of body image.

What Lili described as 'body memories' of being raped were actually hallucinations, a symptom of the worsening Schizoaffective Disorder. She was unable to use physiological or emotional experiences as signals to herself, resulting in the distressing experience of encopresis. She had difficulty differentiating fantasy from reality, internal from external. Her lack of boundaries prevented her from distinguishing self from others.

Lili's dissociation made it difficult to function in her daily life. She frequently felt disoriented and disorganized. Not being consciously aware of her feelings made it impossible to connect intellect and emotion. She could neither think about nor reflect on her feelings. Without the ability to recognize and manage one's feelings, it is impossible to develop a core self and sense of agency.[14] This resulted in Lili feeling totally out of control. Our task together was to decrease the dissociation and to increase Lili's

---

14   Krystal, Henry. (1988)

ability to be aware of and to tolerate feelings, both physical and emotional. Until this was accomplished, Lili's ability to manage her life would be severely impaired.

Lili's medical leave was helpful in a variety of ways. It allowed her to spend time paying attention to her self and it allowed her time to say goodbye to her grandmother. She resumed taking her medications, which increased her "ability to focus without fear" and to make better use of therapy.

• •

My mind, as you may have noticed, had unique connections and responses to life situations. Disconnection came frequently. Emotion and Intellect had very little interaction with one another. Each functioned as if the other did not exist. Intellect got me to work and school. Intellect drove the car. Intellect conversed with people and performed the actions required by the environment. Intellect fooled people into unawareness of the inner me. Intellect separated me from my self.

Emotions horrified me. Mine ran rampant like a thrown super ball bounces. My emotions remained hidden in the presence of people. I know, this sounds contradictory in nature, but it is true. The emotional part was always on the lookout for escape. On occasion, I would stop whatever public activity I was engaged in and go lock myself in the women's restroom. I would lie on the floor with my eyes closed and fists clenched waiting for an inkling of calm before meeting with the public again. Intellect would fight for control. Emotion screamed for control. What a battle.

Often Hannah Lee took the opportunity to remind me I am human. I always groaned and sometimes turned off when she brought this up. Hannah Lee would laugh at my denials. I didn't want to be human; I wanted to be better than human. So often the things she pointed out as parts of my being human were the very things I feared about myself or desired to be rid of in myself.

For example, my desire was not to feel emotion at all. Hannah Lee would tell me that we were made to laugh, cry, become angry, love. She even admitted that she sometimes cried. That amazed me. She is so self-assured and healthy, what could she have to cry about? Hannah Lee is evidently human, too. Now *that* was a bit of a revelation. Hannah Lee completely human? Wow. I, on the other hand, wanted to push my humanity aside. I wanted relationship without human vulnerability. I wanted life with no constraints. I needed to become better than everyone else so that we might be equal. I feared the frailties of being human. Hannah Lee pushed for being human. She wanted me to accept being human in all its ways and manners. Hannah Lee wanted me to be myself and to accept myself. What a thought. What an expectation.

Though I wanted to be better than human, I was desperately and totally human. I proved my being human through the one thing that stayed consistently with me no matter what—my faith in God. I knew God was there carrying me along every agonizing step of the way. The consistent thing about God is that God is strong and stable. He was able to hug me in my head. I could see Him in his white robes with arms spread wide ready to hug and protect, a solid figure in my life. I often relied on God's constancy even as I yelled and screamed at Him. My life wasn't as I'd envisioned it. There was too much pain, loneliness, and confusion. I would rail my fists at God screaming my cries of neediness. Often, I had complained, first to Harry and then to Hannah Lee, that I could not feel love for God. I complained that I felt empty toward him. Harry had said to look for love as an action and not only a feeling. Hannah was quiet on the issue; either that or I fogged out and don't know what she said. No matter how I felt, or didn't, the knowledge of God's saving, steadfast love usually stayed with me. His umbrella of love most likely kept life from bombarding me even more than it did. Still, I must confess to pounding the dirt with great anguish while yelling at and questioning God.

Dear Lord, I need your help today. I cannot take this anymore. I am so far behind, and there seems to be no visible end in sight. I am always in trouble at work. I just can't get the stuff done that needs to be done. I continuously show my boss how unworthy I am. I cannot do this anymore, God. Help me, please. Oh, God, help me.

Why is it that I believe in you yet do not trust you? I have got to put my full trust in you, yet I don't. I don't trust myself either.

Why can I not be passionate about something so that I can immerse myself in your Word or love? I cannot immerse myself in teaching and all the damn paperwork. I cannot immerse myself in my writing or in other things. I want to quit Lord. Oh, how I want to quit. I want to become a blob of an unknown quantity that no one can see or feel or hear or touch. Perhaps that is what I already am. But no, if that were true, I would not be feeling the pain and fear and guilt I feel. Please God, rescue me. I am crying with all the pain. and yet the tears do not fall.

Can't I just quit life Lord? Can't I? Well, it is time to pretend to teach, so I must go. Goodbye, Lord, goodbye.

I have lain here crying my eyes out because Harry called to tell me he is still praying for me. I am not a nothing to Harry. I am not just a file, I am a something; a something worth praying for. At least to Harry.

I am tired of people telling me what I like.

I am tired of hearing voices and noise in my head. I am tired of not being able to focus. I am tired of discussing the abuse of my students. I am tired of not being able to think without a jumbled head. I am angry and scared, and I want to cry. I am ugly.

One of the first battles between Hannah Lee and me revolved around prayer. I wanted her to pray for me during sessions. Harry used to pray, therefore, I expected the same from Hannah Lee. We were all Christians. Don't Christians pray for one another? Hannah Lee did not believe in prayer on demand. She didn't want to be ordered to pray. I didn't think I was ordering her to pray. I was begging for her to pray. Hannah Lee told me I could pray during sessions. But, I wanted to be taken care of. I wanted to be cared about. If Hannah Lee wouldn't pray for me, she couldn't possibly care for me. This battle went on for months, maybe even years. I don't remember. One day I asked Hannah Lee if she ever prayed for clients. She said yes she did, but privately, not on demand. Another boundary. Another fuel for my anger. I was afraid to ask her if she ever prayed for me. What if she said no?

I needed to know God was on my side. My first memory of God being in my life was in third grade. I remember making a picture with dried beans during Vacation Bible School, and suddenly I discovered and met God. In this meeting, I knew I had known Him all my life. He was not a surprise. He hadn't had a name, but there had always been an envelope of care surrounding me that I couldn't define and which was separate from the care I felt from my family. And suddenly, during third grade, I knew.

Knowing God has been a journey filled with confidence and angst. A part of me always knows He is there, loving and protecting. I do my best to acknowledge and thank Him for every positive in my life. I have even thanked Him for my emotional difficulties. They've given me a compassion for people who are hurting I otherwise might not have. My passion in the world of hurting people is the young children. My heart cries out to them and for them. I thank God for this passion.

My screams, my Lord,
are screams of passion
I cry out in my soul
I want to love you with all my heart
But can I?

I want so much to be on bended knee
I want to bow down before you.
I ache with yearning
I wish to pour out my soul to you

But, God, it isn't happening
I fear my bended knees
I fear what I would discover, my Lord
I fear what I would discover

But not about you.
You are Love, Compassion,
You are everything human
and everything eternal
You are I AM.

What I fear, my Lord,
is me
what I would discover of me
in the torrid blackness that I fear
and do not yet know
It is there, Lord
and in it I fear

I wish to confess, Lord,
and do not know what to confess
I wish to bow before you,
and honor your I AMness
But I fear myself.
It is I who gets in the way

Love me Lord,
Love me to my knees
Love me to trust you
Love me Lord.
Love me.

Then there's the flip side. I remember one summer when I sank down onto the dirt and flung my fists at God for all the hurt and pain within me. There was no one but me and God. I screamed. I yelled. I pounded my fists into the dirt. Overwhelmed with emotion, I lashed out at God. Through the years there would be many episodes where I ranted and raved at God, at his Son. My ranting never asked, "Why me?" I yelled and begged for the pain to go away. I begged for his love and protection.

Sometimes I could feel myself surrounded by his arms and glistening white robes. There was this place just outside the safe room Mandy helped me build where I could be on a large round rock near a trickling stream. The sun would shine down, its rays of light streaming down to surround me, bouncing off the water like glitter. In the midst of this beauty, God would come in his flowing white robe, arms outstretched. His arms encircled me, and for that moment I felt loved, safe. Sometimes I would simply sink luxuriously into the moment. At other times, my tears would pour forth in numbers too great to count.

Within my deepest despair, I turned to Psalm 77:1-2:

I cried out to God for help
I cried out to God to hear me.
When I was in distress,
I sought the Lord:
at night I stretched out
untiring hands
and my soul refused to be
comforted.

This Psalm spoke my anguish when I could think of no other words; they told God I was not to be comforted no matter what. The words also reminded me that I was connected to God no matter what, and that, ironically, brought me comfort.

How I longed for my God when I felt all alone. How I yearned. Yet, no matter how horrible my life or I was, somewhere inside me was always the knowledge that God was there in all his glorious magnificent love.

Where am I, God
Where am I
I want to love you with my heart and soul,
But where am I, God, where am I

There is life all around me God
You are that life
I long to praise you with all my heart and soul
But where am I God, where am I

I've seen you, God, in my daily strife
I've felt you in my pain
I discover your footsteps all through my life
But where am I, God, where am I

Oh, God, my God, you are meant to be the passion of my life
You are the awesome Creator, the Savior
Oh, God, my God, your majesty awes all mortals
And in this God, where am I?

You have woven a tapestry, my God
a tapestry of goodness, and pain,
a tapestry so simple and yet complex
I know this tapestry my Lord, I feel it
I see it in my soul and heart
But, where am I oh God, where am I?

As I seek your Glory and feel my pain
I sense your presence so near to my heart
I feel your arms so strong, so steady
I find the cloth of your robes keeping me warm
I smell the sweet fragrance of protection
Where am I, God, Where am I?

And then I know.
I am in your arms.
The arms of protection.
The arms of love.

Where am I, God, where am I?
Why, I am with you!

Occasionally, our church is filled with a labyrinth. It is this huge mat on the floor that looks like a maze. The labyrinth may look like a maze, but in actuality it has only a single path to follow. The idea behind walking along the labyrinth is to pray and focus upon God. It can be a very powerful experience.

I walked the labyrinth. It was a painful experience. I wanted a mind open to the Lord. I wanted my mind open to His voice. I wanted answers to so very many questions. I wanted to clear my mind of excessive thought and commune with God. Instead, I felt all the pain of the experience. I filled with the angst I felt about God. I shared how I don't know how to love him. I shared that I don't know for sure that he loves me. I shared that I don't know what it means to love him. I was filled with a great deal of pain. I cried. I wanted to cry harder, and if I had been alone I would have filled the place with wails of wanting. I became confused about whether I was hearing God speak to me or if it were myself speaking to me. I didn't find any answers. I didn't feel soothed by God. In the center of the labyrinth, I lay prostrate and God (or me) told me to put my pain into a box, gift wrap it, and give it to him. I did that in my mind to the best of my ability. My body is so very tense and tight right now. I am also very exhausted from the experience. I would do it again. I needed to spend more time there than I did, but didn't want to hold my friend back as she had finished the labyrinth several minutes before I did. I am very tired.

For a time, when I felt void of all emotion, I became ashamed and frightened. I could not find love in my heart for God, for Christ. Instead, I felt empty. During that session with Harry when I moaned and groaned about this seeming inability to feel love for God, he went through the Bible showing me verses and stories where love was an action, not a feeling. This didn't help me much because, dammit, I wanted to feel!

What a mix-up my emotions were, I either felt bombarded by every emotion at once, or I felt empty, completely empty. Yet, somewhere within me there must have been a working trust of, and a working faith in, God and within this subconscious belief came a seed of protection against all that my mind couldn't handle. God protected me and loved me despite myself. Looking back I see this so well.

One struggle I dealt with was whether or not mental illness was a sin. This was an especially important question during my years of studying counseling at a Christian school. It might have been my own misunderstanding, but I kept hearing one particular professor saying that mental illness is a sin. Whether the professor ever really said this or not, the questions this brought forth tormented my brain. While I acknowledged that I was a sinner, I couldn't equate that with an illness being a sin. After much fretful pondering, I finally reached the conclusion that the mental illness itself was not a sin. My understanding of sin was that it was anything that we do that separates us from God. In my mental illness, I was often far from a relationship with God. To me, the sin would not be having a mental illness, but in not doing anything about it if the person had any capacity to work his or her way out of it.

Fully Human

Lili vacillated between feeling "bombarded" by her feelings and feeling "empty." In her words, "Emotions horrified me." She wished to be more than human, yet felt less than human. When she thought of Harry praying for her, she thought "I am not a nothing—I am a something." Feeling like "something" allowed Lili to objectify herself and to avoid her humanity. Instead of a "something," I wanted Lili to acknowledge that she was "someone"—a fully human being with fully human feelings. If we refuse to own our humanity by distancing ourselves from our human feelings, we become unable to experience our love for God and His love for us.

It is not possible for human beings to exist without feelings. We can't cause our feelings to cease to be. The most we can do in this regard is to deny them and defend against them, in which case they can become so powerful that they can break through our defenses and overwhelm us. Thus, Lili was left feeling empty or feeling bombarded. When she was overwhelmed with feelings, she became confused, disorganized and unable to think. In order to stop feeling overwhelmed by her intense feelings, Lili had to develop the capacity to tolerate her feelings and to use them productively. The only way to accomplish this was to acknowledge her feelings as an acceptable part of her self. Through accepting her feelings, it was possible for Lili to learn to regulate them and use them as signals. She could begin to integrate feelings and thinking. Lili could acknowledge her humanity and could quit being afraid of what she might discover about herself.

Lili "wanted a mind open to the Lord." But an open mind is not enough. The first of all the commandments is, "Thou shalt love the Lord thy God with all thy heart and with all thy soul and with all thy mind and with all thy strength."[15] To me this indicates that love is action, but also more than action. It involves feelings as well as thoughts and action. In order to be all that God requires of us, we must first accept our humanity. Only then can we love God with our whole heart, soul, mind, and strength.

Lili wondered if mental illness is sin. I think she is right when she says, "the sin would not be having a mental illness, but in not doing anything about it if I had any capacity to work my way out of it."

• •

---

15   Luke 10:27; *Holy Bible*. King James Version.

Twenty-six

Speaking of God brings me to the subjects of suicide and death. I spent a great part of my young adulthood fearing death. This fear came alive when I would close my eyes. All I would see was opaque blackness filled with dirt and an empty eyeless skull. Worms crawled along my skinless bones in an ever-present existence. In this picture, I became nothing. No body. No soul. Just claustrophobic dirt.

It was through my grandparents that I learned about death, especially my grandmothers. Death can be a good thing when the time is right and when you have positive expectations. Grandma P. loved Jesus. In this love she was a sweet gentle spirit, very prim and proper. Grandma P. attended church and Sunday School every Sunday. She loved sitting at her piano playing and singing hymns. I once painted a picture of a church on a piece of cardboard. She placed it above the piano where it stayed until she entered a nursing home. Grandma P. had some memory problems in her later years. Most likely it was Alzheimer's. She loosened up a bit in a very charming way. She even told me a naughty joke. I don't remember the joke, but love the memory. When Grandma P. passed away, she did so joyously, glad to finally meet her Jesus. Grandma P. was beautiful and peaceful in her death. When I saw her in her coffin, I knew: death does not need to be feared. I thank Grandma P. for taking away my fear of death. It is lovely to remember her.

From her deathbed, Grandma M. gave me one final glimpse of the power of love. It was the evening before her passing. Grandma M. had been in a catatonic state for several days. I got a phone call saying that she was probably going to die in the next day or so. This, of course, rushed me to her side to spend some time and say goodbye. When I got there, Grandma was lying still staring into space. I took her hand and began talking and singing to her. She never moved. Eyes straight ahead, body still, arms at her side. I couldn't even tell if she were breathing or not, she was that still. When I got no reaction from her, I told Grandma M. that if she wanted me to stay to squeeze my hand. Joy filled my heart when I felt the tiniest bit of pressure or movement. Grandma wanted me to stay. I talked and sang for a while longer. I told her that even though I would miss her, it was okay for her to go. Then I made my heart's desire known.

"Grandma," I said. "I wish you would look at me just one more time." My heart stood still as I waited. My heart leaped with joy when I saw her eyes struggling, and then it happened. Grandma's eyes moved. They made contact with mine. The sort of contact where you know you have seen one another. It lasted less than a second, but it happened. Grandma M. saw me one last time, and I saw my grandma. She passed away in the early hours of the next day. I didn't cry when Grandma M. died, but I struggled with the loss. Sometime after the funeral some of us stopped by Grandma's house and talked our way in. It was a bit of relief to see that so much remodeling had been done by the new owner that it was no longer in any respect Grandma M's house. Because of all the remodeling and the bicycle tracks on the common area walls (Grandma never rode her bicycle on the wall), it didn't feel as if Grandma's house were being invaded. It is hard to invade something that no longer exists.

A few months later, when Princess Diana died, I cried my buckets of tears over the loss of my Grandma M. Hannah Lee says that Grandma's death was hard for me. But, I think most of my grief and pain happened before she died. Her death brought sorrow. The loss of her house brought devastation, panic, and fear. The result of these events was a loneliness of spirit. I really don't remember much about this time period. I don't remember my actual thoughts and feelings of the time—at least not about Grandma's death. It was the house I mourned. Odd, isn't it?

My first encounter with death was when Grandpa W. died in that very same house decades before. I was about eight years old. For years I had recurring dreams of his still being alive and that he had never died. In one dream, my real grandpa comes off an airplane and I burst into joy because my real grandpa is back, not the dead one whose blue eyes stared at me from his coffin. (His eyes were not really open, but I have always remembered them as such. I would swear Grandpa W. stared at me when I saw him in his coffin.) The other dream was so real that I was an adult before I would go freely into Grandma's bathroom. In this dream, Grandpa was alive and living in the shower behind the shower curtain. Since I didn't believe Grandpa was dead, and yet I was fearful that he was, I was terrified of whomever was behind that shower curtain. No. I did not go in that bathroom for a

164 ～ **Kelly Ann Compton**

couple of decades by choice. If I were sent in there for something, I didn't look toward the shower. I was fearful that my dream would come true and Grandpa would step out of that shower. I was more fearful that he wouldn't. Thankfully my two grandmas would change my view of death. True, with no fear of death, suicide might have appeared more desirable—I mean, who wouldn't want to meet Jesus? Sounded like a fair trade to me and a perfectly happy ending. However, in reality and in my craziness, suicide never appeared as pretty or as inviting as the intrusive voice gave to it.

Hannah Lee had something to do with this. She threatened to dump me if I ended up in the hospital. My perception. What Hannah Lee really told me was that she didn't "do hospitals" anymore. Having lost Harry due to one hospital stay, I wasn't about to let Hannah Lee abandon me so easily. My fear of abandonment evidently had more hold over my actions than the push to kill myself, for I was never hospitalized again.

Still, I was often filled with suicidal ideation. Knives terrified the not-so-suicidal part of me. Most often I would envision shredding the skin off my face and body. Frequently I would stare at a wall along the road wanting to ram into it, and sometimes made that initial move. Something, or Someone, would stop me from following through with the act. When it was over, I would be shaking and sweating, or laughing with a maniacal glee at what wasn't.

I don't think I ever actually wanted the death aspect of suicide. Suicide was viewed as the safe and fast way to freedom. What I wanted was to be free. Free from pain, anger, fear, and my dark unknown horribleness. Death meant freedom from all that held me in that horrifying place of confusion. I ached to be free from brain pain. I ached for a feeling of lightness and buoyancy. I ached to be free from this mess that supposedly constituted me. It is difficult thinking of this space, a bit frightening, actually. At the time, the thought of nonexistence was comforting. Now, it seems unimaginable to even wish for such a thing.

While I never actually followed through with plans of suicide, the plans were always there. Most of the time, the voice of the plans was not mine. Someone else, who chose to remain nameless, most often told me what the plan was. Drive into the wall. Drive off a cliff. Set the house on fire. Slice my face into smithereens. I think what saved me during these moments was the perception that someone else was giving the orders. I came closest to actual damage when the thoughts were definitely mine. Scratching myself, drawing blades across my arms, holding scissors points at my throat with increasing pressure. At one point I gave many sharp objects to a friend to hold for me until their spell over me was broken. To this day I will not own a pizza cutter. No way. Evidently, that spell has not been broken.

Suicide was the only way I knew to get away from my perceived terribleness, from the confusion, from all those bits and pieces of junk that flashed continually through my head. Thoughts of suicide became a cycle traveling through my brain. Sometimes it seemed that the thoughts were always present. At other times suicide niggled at my brain without blazing onto the big screen. And once in awhile, I had no such thoughts at all. Those were nice freeing moments.

Evidently, some part of me, or one of my mes, did not desire death, for here I am and glad of it. I do look forward to the day I get to meet Jesus face to face, but I will do that in His time, not mine. Hallelujah to life! No longer do I plan death or invite it to come my way. Death will come in its own time, in God's time.

It is through my own overpowering suicidal ideation and thoughts that I have some sort of understanding of those women who killed their children to save them. Invasion of thought so overwhelming and powerful can lead to serious sad endings. Looking at my own inability to take control over the voices and actions of the people inside me, I understand knowing that doing a certain action is wrong, yet also having the overwhelming compulsion that it must be done. My whole mental illness was tortured by the inability to differentiate between real and not-real. Within this frame of mind, knowing right from wrong can exist alongside the inability to ignore or inhibit some horrible action. How sad for those women.

No Escape

I've often seen clients who are terrified of falling into a traumatic state in which they experience unbearable emotional and autonomic arousal. In such a state, there is no sense of time and clients report feeling that there is no escape from the horrific experience. They express the fear of this traumatic state as a fear that they are going to die.

Lili shares with us that she spent much of her young adulthood fearing death. Why would that be? Just as she felt bombarded by emotions as an adult, it is likely that in her early life she had experienced powerful affects that she could neither control nor escape. Such overwhelming affects would have been accompanied by physiological overstimulation and a sense of helplessness to escape it. As an adult, unconsciously dreading a return to this state could be interpreted as a fear of death.[16]

When infants are overstimulated, a parent intervenes to soothe them. In therapy, this parental function is replaced by the soothing presence of another adult who understands: the therapist. Prior to Lili's being able to utilize the support and containment offered through therapy, death (suicide) was the only way she could imagine getting away from the overwhelming feelings and confusion she often experienced. In her words, "Death meant freedom from all that held me in that horrifying place of confusion." Thus, for Lili, death was both a fear and a wish.

Lili's psychic trauma was presymbolic, meaning that she had no words to express it. My job was to understand and reflect her feelings accurately through the countertransference experienced in therapy. I then had to begin to help her find words for the feelings and to encourage her to begin to be aware of what she was thinking and feeling. As therapy progressed, she became more and more able to tolerate and to verbalize feelings. This contributed to her emotional growth and to her developing a sense of self.

By the way—I didn't threaten to "dump" Lili if she ended up in the hospital. Because I was no longer doing inpatient work, I did tell her I would refer her to another psychologist for hospitalization if needed. I would, however, have continued to see her after she was discharged and able to be safe. Fortunately, Lili was able to use this boundary as a way of dealing with issues *before* she became so overwhelmed that she required hospitalization.

• •

16   KRYSTAL, HENRY. (1988)

Twenty-seven

A pleasant surprise occurred Sunday. I used a rotary blade to cut some paper for a project I was doing. Toward the end of the project, it dawned on me: Not once was I afraid of the rotary blade. Not once did I see it as an instrument of mutilation and a sign of my coming death. How strange it felt, that lack of threat and fear, that lack of hypnotic desire. On Sunday, my rotary blade became merely a cloth and paper cutting instrument. That is really a rather relaxing and relieving thought.

Fighting and Chasing Sanity

Recovery itself has been an interesting journey. I fought it with passion. I fought sanity with a passion. Yet, I hated the world I was living in. The thought of choosing sanity was too confusing. I was afraid of the unknown. Separating what was real for other people from what was real for me felt like an insurmountable task. Yet, somewhere inside, I knew I had to fight the craziness.

I did not know how to be a normal healthy person. When I was no longer bombarded with intense nonstop emotion, I thought I no longer had any emotion. I believed myself now to feel nothing. "Listen," Hannah Lee would say, "listen to your body." She would have me tell her the physical sensations I was experiencing and would then suggest an emotion I might be feeling. Freedom from all that attacking emotion made me feel dead rather than free. Interesting. Slowly I became accustomed to the more normal range of emotion and therefore, more able to recognize that yes, I was feeling something, and yes, I knew what it might be.

Recovery meant that the relationship with Hannah Lee would end someday. In my head, someday was never. I was adamant that we continue. Hannah Lee said sure and proceeded to begin her first excursion as Ms. Famous World Traveler. Okay, so she's not really famous.

I continued to become fearful and resentful whenever Hannah Lee's life outside our time interfered with our time together. What if I needed her? What if I blew up into little pieces while she was out gallivanting around? I would hibernate in my bed for fear of what would happen while Hannah Lee was out of town. I would call her voice mail constantly to reassure myself with her voice. Just the sound of her voice brought a bit of soothing calmness.

Everything is changing. EVERYTHING. Hannah Lee is slowly leaving. Bit by bit she is stealing furniture away from her office. Slowly she is allowing her client numbers to dwindle. Week by week changes come about over which I have no control. It is deja vu. Grandma's house was gone before Grandma died and I was ready to say goodbye, and now the same thing is happening. Before I am ready to say goodbye to Hannah Lee, the office and all it represents are disappearing before my very eyes. The grieving process must begin once again. The place of total acceptance is about to disappear. Oh yeah, life is looking good.

I am afraid to have enthusiasm for life, afraid of ever having enthusiastic energy. At the same time, I yearn for enthusiasm and energy. I want to love life. I want to be filled with such enthusiasm that I can't wait to do life. Enthusiastic energy would lead to joy and contentment. It would allow a love for life. I would be able to do the volunteer work I want to do. My dream of organizing a children's haven could be realized. Oh, what I could do with a bit of long-term enthusiasm and energy! Sigh. Herein lies the problem: Enthusiasm and energy bring on contentment, which requires commitment and responsibility. My brain wears out just thinking about such pressure. Then the fear steps in and being a healthy, energetic person does not seem possible. Nor does it seem worthwhile. It is too much work.

Still, I can feel my mental health improving. Sometimes it feels as fresh as a springtime breeze. Energy has begun soaring through my body. I don't recall ever feeling this alive! I come home from work and still have energetic vitality ready to clean or play. My bed and television no longer demand my presence when I walk in the door. Is this what life is like for most people?

I wonder. What is the reality of living? Does the reality of life change from day to day? Will I ever return to the voices' control or that depressing steam shovel? Do I have to take medication for the rest of my life?

The first time Hannah Lee left the country, I was so caught up in my fear and worry I couldn't admit that I was actually handling her extended absence with relative ease. I had not yet noticed that my mode of being had become much calmer and more stable. I was no longer in constant crisis. The voices had dimmed quite a bit. My mind relaxed now and then. Medication and therapy were proving their worth. Yes, I was much better. Still, the fear was there. And guess what? I made it. I didn't want to, but I did. I survived the absence of my anchor. Was I, perhaps, beginning to form my own anchor?

Today, there were no voices
Today, there was no fading
Today, there was no swirling
Today, there was freedom of clarity
Today, there was fun.
Today, I was a child among children!

For a long time after things began clearing up inside of me, I didn't realize that the relative quietness growing within me was a more normal state of being. You would think getting well would be a good thing. It is. Sometimes. I was not a mass of confusing emotions anymore with all the extremes of each and every emotion. Life became more the ripples on a lake rather than Hurricane Hugo. Healthy mental health is a good thing, but it has its drawbacks. For instance, being healthy meant I would lose my therapist. She was the one person in the world I allowed to hear my confusion, my darkness, my terror of being human. All the horrors of being me had been released into the gentle safe haven of her office. I never wanted to leave, ever. Each week as our hour drew to a close, I would curl up with fear, tears welling, and fists clenched. I wanted to stay in the safety of her figurative arms where no harm could reach me. It had been six years, and still every week, I resisted facing the confusing, terrifying world outside her office. Every week she reminded me that I could come back the next week. Every week I didn't believe her. Every week I counted on her.

As a few more years went by, there proved to be less and less reason to be in therapy. The horrors of life were lessening day by day, week by week. Only one terror truly remained. That of leaving my therapist. The horror, the fear in my heart of not being in that safest of places with the safest of people, paralyzed me. If she left town or changed an appointment I was positive she was trying to get rid of me. There waited within me a terrifying fear that my therapist would abandon me.

My brain felt lost and empty. Where was all the noise? I didn't feel confused but was convinced that I was now an empty shell. At the same time I felt suddenly free. Free to learn about me. Free to become me. The freedom felt grand! It was a bit like the oohing and aahing over the first time the Christmas tree lights are turned on. Peaceful and beautiful. A bit of heaven on earth, actually. The freedom of normalcy also allowed me to see the world in a much clearer light. I learned that even people who have not been in crazy mode have problems and fears and "stuff." I was sometimes able to hear their pain now. I was able to see that being normal did not mean being without concerns. This new perspective certainly added to my freedom of thought. It opened up the world of normalcy. Okay, I can feel happy and joyful. I can allow myself to feel sadness or anger. Even more important is the freedom to actually recognize my feelings and not be afraid of them. I don't always know what to do with my feelings, but I don't hide from them either. Yes, having a more normal framework for being was freeing.

I don't think there is a tunnel anymore. I haven't seen or visited those dark caverns in a long while. An old movie I saw every year in school was "Donald Duck In Mathmagic Land." In this film, we're given a look inside Donald's brain. What a mess! There were overstuffed file cabinets, cobwebs and dust, and files piled in disarray. That is what my brain once felt like. After a good sweeping, Donald's brain is clear, neat, organized, and no longer filled with cobwebs. This is how my brain now feels.

My brain stores so much information that it becomes periodically overwhelmed and hides things from me. Sometimes it is the present situation; other times it is memories from the past. As I write this in the present tense I wonder: Do I still fog out? Does my brain still hide things from me? The answer, I believe, is very seldom. When it does happen it happens in a different manner and intensity. When I fog out it is more in the nature of daydreaming than dissociating from pain and anger. Strange things might happen on occasion, but they are no longer fearful. I know I am generally clearheaded these days. I can usually tell what is real and what is not. I am so glad. There are sporadic moments when I am not sure where something in my brain came from: Dream, real, or imaginary, but it is nothing like those years of total confusion.

Day by day, week by week, Lili could feel herself gaining peace and strength and calmness. Life's daily stresses were no longer powerful killers. The medication was working. Lili would find therapy sessions empty of the need to purge madness or thought. She knew the time was coming when therapy would no longer be cost-effective. Cost-effective. This was the intellectual rationale of her mind. She didn't want to stop seeing Hannah Lee. Ever. They were so much alike in Lili's eye. She wished they could be friends. Lili refused to quit therapy, because if she did, she would never see Hannah Lee again. Hannah Lee had told her this from the start, "We can never be friends. We cannot have a relationship outside the therapeutic relationship." Bah. Humbug. Lili had a plan. She would become so entrenched in Hannah Lee's life—I mean heart—that Hannah Lee would break her stupid rules and become friends with her. Now, however, Lili was becoming worried. Therapy was winding down. Lili was accepting her humanity. Her fears were no longer engulfing her soul. And Hannah Lee was still just a therapist. Lili did not in any way want to believe this. She needed Hannah Lee. She wanted to need Hannah Lee. Forever. Lili was so angry over this one remaining issue. It was not really the only issue; it was merely the most prominent issue containing rage and fear and sadness. Every emotion Lili had ever dealt with was contained in this one snowballing issue. Lili did not want to say goodbye to Hannah Lee. Lili would not say good bye to Hannah Lee. Not if she didn't have to ...

I brought my fear of leaving therapy and Hannah Lee to her attention. She reassured me that when it was time to end therapy, most people knew and were ready. She assured me that I could always go back and that she wouldn't desert me. The fear I had was in never seeing Hannah Lee ever again. I still hold that fear to some extent even though I know where to find her. Another fear was that she would forget me. I determined that I was not important enough to be remembered. Hannah Lee would ask me if I remembered people or thought about them. I said yes, but insisted that it was different, that I was not important enough to be remembered. There were many other people more worthwhile to take up space in Hannah Lee's head than me.

It took awhile, but in discovering that I had a self and that that self is rather likable, useful and worth remembering, being separated from Hannah Lee was not nearly as traumatic as my insides thought it would be. Perhaps Hannah Lee's first steps toward becoming Ms. Famous World Traveler took away some of that fear. I mean, she always came back; she never forgot me. She gave me a sense of worth, and she demonstrated to me that I was valued. Hannah Lee didn't throw me away or disappear. She simply lived her life and encouraged me to live mine.

Recovery was not without its pitfalls. Nothing is ever smooth it seems. There were still those waves of ugliness popping up in the midst of it all.

This weekend has been miserable. My eyes look red and swollen as if I have been crying all weekend. I have not. I have felt back in the clutches of depression and feelings I haven't felt in a long time. It is an overwhelming feeling of ick. I sit in my car and scream outrageous things at people. I can't get motivated to do much. I feel oppressed by my own brain. Hannah Lee would ask me what has been going on. This was supposed to be a good weekend with two parties to attend. I went to one. The other I canceled out on. How did this start? It is as if a click happens in my brain. Click. And the depression comes. Click. And the feeling of oppression comes. Click. And I can't enjoy myself. I have spent the weekend in a lamenting mood. I wanted to call Hannah Lee, but didn't because she would want me to try to overcome it by myself. Perhaps I have. Anyway, I feel that I am improving. Perhaps tomorrow will be better.

Now hope remained a bit more realistic. The bouts with depression could end with hope rather than visions of destruction. The people inside me were able to rest and disappear from constant bothersome noise.

Still, getting well, healthy, is a battle. Admitting you are well can also be a battle. For after almost twelve years of therapy, you are not sure you can handle life without a therapist. The therapist becomes the anchor of survival. Even if not in the forefront of one's brain, the knowledge that every week you'll get to be in the safe cocoon of her presence keeps you sane. You are not sure you can make it without your therapist.

It is a scary proposition that idea of going it alone. Growing pains. Leaving home. That's what it is. Leaving home. It is the baby being separated from mom. It is moving from a safe crawl to that possibly dangerous run.

I felt like Peter Pan never wanting to grow up and move into that scary world of adulthood where you are all alone with no one to pick you up. I feared being out there all alone without the cocoon, without my anchor, without the safety.

No matter, recovery kept up its ever increasing pace. It was almost as if I were slowly snowballing toward health rather than insanity.

FULLY ALIVE!

The goal of therapy is always termination, and termination comes with its own pitfalls and process. It is to be expected that during the termination process there is a certain amount of anxiety, and anxiety causes regression. In Lili's case, she wondered, "What if I blew up into little pieces?" You may recall that she had addressed this issue early on when watching "Carrie" on television. Lili had realized, "It could not really happen that way." And, she was able to recognize fairly quickly this time around that, of course, she was not going to blow up into little pieces.

In addition to regression, an important part of termination is going through a grief process. Termination is related to the loss of a significant relationship in your life, and anger and sadness are a part of that loss. Grieving allows separation and individuation to occur. While the external "place of total acceptance" is disappearing, it is an opportunity to recognize that you have internalized the sense of safety and security that have been present in that external place.

Lili had been afraid of life. She recognized that being fully alive requires commitment and responsibility, which she sometimes saw as "too much work." Yet she also wanted the freedom to be her own self. While she had entered therapy with the idea "*You'd best take good care of me,*" she was now faced with the knowledge that being healthy meant not only she would lose her therapist, but also that she would be responsible for taking care of herself. She would have to use her feelings as signals about her own needs and desires rather than to control others to take care of her (which had not worked well anyway!). The opposite of fear is faith. I had faith in Lili's ability to be herself and take care of her self. and Lili was beginning to have faith in her self as well!

· ·

Twenty-eight

It didn't happen over night. I mean, it wasn't like one day I was a normal human being and the next day I woke up nuts. That is not how it happened. The process of becoming crazy evolved over time. I can remember bits and pieces of craziness throughout my growing up years. The fantasies of spanking machines made of 2x4s and having the sharp ends of nails sticking out. The constant fear of people finding out about my insides—about who I really was. The poems of dark, eerie, mistrustful thoughts. My aloneness.

My aloneness was necessity. How could I possibly be a contributing member of any given group without my aloneness? Being with people was usually nerve-wracking.

By the way, I am not crazy! Oh what an important statement of belief. How many years of therapy it has taken for me to be able to say, write and think that statement with belief. I AM NOT CRAZY. I can even smile about it all now. I felt crazy for years. It was only with the onset of a broken heart that I acknowledged my craziness and let others in on it.

In the glow of my recovery of stable mind and emotional health, I could look back and view some things in a different light with a more "normal" perspective. My ability to discern the answers to the "real not-real" questions was greatly improved. I became able to look back at the previous decade and admit to events being hallucinations rather than actual events. For example, the body memories. Now *those* were hallucinations. There was no man doing sexual things to me. The things I felt, tasted, and smelled were not really there. At the time, those body memories were as real to me as the house I lived in. Now, I know they were hallucinations. But, I still wonder if there is some real-life basis for them, whatever that may be.

I am thinking about the sexual abuse. I spent years trying to figure out who the perpetrator was. I begged Hannah Lee to answer my questions about the abuse. "Hypnotize me, help me find the answers," I cried. Hannah Lee said that if the memories were real, they would become clearer on their own. Also, survival in the present was of greater concern. Eventually, I came to terms with the fact that I may never know, and had, in fact, forgiven that unknown person. As years passed and I grew stronger, a new thought crept into my mind. Were the memories of sexual abuse real or just more hallucinations? This thought was a bit of a shocker. I may never know. There came an agreement with Hannah Lee that there was nothing in my current life where such answers were necessary. I feel very blessed that none of my therapists led me into false beliefs—they didn't fall into that "false memory dilemma" so many therapists have placed themselves and their clients in. While things could happen in life that would push the possible sexual abuse to the forefront of my life, for now I am content to let the issue lie fallow.

Some people might insist that something truly horrific must have happened for me to have such a long difficult journey through mental illness. I am here to say that, yes, bad things happened. Every life has the not-so-hot side. I am sure these "bad" things affected me somehow, but I am more certain that the mental illness can be more accurately accounted for by my brain's unique reactions to everyday life experiences.

I wondered: Why was I one of the lucky ones to develop a mental illness? Hmmmm ... My hunch is that it was not so much about things that had happened to me, but in how my personality perceived things. I remember often feeling unheard. There was this tension of wanting and hiding. I have always wanted someone to know the real me, yet have hidden the real me from everyone I know, myself included. It was just too dangerous to let people know about me. Also, I didn't know me for sure. As I write this, I can tell you that I am intelligent, sturdy and steady, goal oriented, and a survivor.

In more recent times, a chemical imbalance in the brain has been accepted as one part of mental illness. This, I believe. Various circumstances may have tripped the wire that set off the explosion of emotional havoc, but it was my brain's reaction that kept the explosion recurring. Because of the chemical basis, medication has been a part of the answer. I feel very lucky that my psychiatrist was able to discover the right meds with relative ease. Friends of mine have been through a myriad of drug combinations in search of the right fit, and some have yet to find the right combination. I have been lucky.

Twenty-nine

Sharing the story of my mental illness with you has been important. The generally healthy population doesn't always understand that mental illness is a journey that comes to the most ordinary of people and doesn't necessarily last forever.

The joy of coming out of that tunnel of darkness can be brighter than the sun some days and scarier than the familiar comfort of distress other days.

At times, I feel as if part of my creativity has disappeared. It is as if I need to search for that part of me, rather than having a pressure of creativity at my fingertips. I wonder at this seeming loss. Is it the medication? Do I need to have voices and people inside of me to retrieve my creativity with ease? Or, do I simply need to define or find my creativity in a different way? Perhaps my creative nature is not missing at all. Perhaps it is similar to when my emotions became more normal, and I felt empty until I got use to the calmness.

I feel that I am in pretty good shape these days with much to smile about. My body-listening skills are much improved. I feel emotions at a more moderate level rather than at either extreme. No longer do I need an ever ready escape plan. I can go to a party and not have to hibernate in the corner fearful that someone will expect conversation from me. Finally, people can greet me with a "How are you?" and I don't freak out internally trying to come up with an answer. Life is good.

The truth of the matter is that I was never insane or crazy. There were times when I felt insane and crazy, but I wasn't. Believe you me, having people live inside your head, not being able to differentiate between internal/external or me/you does make a person feel crazy and insane. It also seems perfectly logical at the time and does not allow one to be dissuaded from the perceptions. Perhaps a hundred years ago, crazy and insane would have been the right words for what ailed me. With new knowledge, technology and medications what constitutes crazy and insane must surely be defined differently now.

I do feel blessed and lucky at having the right people at the right time in my life, and this means more than the therapists. It includes family and friends. New lasting friendships developed during this growing process. I discovered I was not alone. I became able to share with my family and not feel as if the knowledge would be a burden. There is much to be grateful for.

My family knew very little of what I now share with you. I did not want them to worry or feel bad. I know and knew they loved me and wanted the best for me. My gift to them was to hide as much of my garbage from them as possible. I don't know whether they would consider this a gift or even a gift they would want, but it was something I had to do. For me, for them.

I have felt very blessed within my state of mental illness. No matter how little or how much people knew of my tribulations, they were always supportive. No one ever put me down or dropped their relationship with me because of knowledge of my so-called craziness. God's grace does live within so many special people. He gave me the gift of relationships that I couldn't see until later. Relationship of unconditional love and care. When I think back I am in awe of all this acceptance. It is incredible how people believed in me and cared about me when I had no hope for my own existence. I look back in amazement. Now, realizing that people were seeing a scary side of me and still supporting me, I feel honored, important. People actually cared for me. In my clenching need to be loved, I was. Wondrous.

While I was still seeing Harry I gave a talk at church one Sunday on my journey of depression. I was filled with trepidation and a bit of fear to be "spilling my guts" in front of these very conservative Christians. Would they banish me from the church? That was my fear. When the service was over, I learned that there were many pain-filled people within those church walls. Several women came up to me, thanking me for my words. Others expressed feeling encouraged and that I had given them hope. That felt good. It also surprised me. My pain and I had helped others in some small way. God truly does amazing things through his people. Amazing stuff.

Support came from every angle through a variety of people. Pastors agreed to be ready to help if I found myself in crisis. Friends gave time and encouragement. I was part of a women's prayer group where I met women who inspired. I have since developed a close relationship with one of these women. Alice lives and breathes her beautiful faith. What a gift she is!

My graduate program required participation in a group therapy experience. I selected the summer version, which was three or four hours a day for two four-day weeks. Ironically, and thankfully, this group took place during the summer of noise and growing craziness. The leader of this group was a woman of intense compassion. This led to group members extending their own compassion. It was the best group I had ever been involved in. Without their knowing it, the members of this group experience helped me contain myself a bit and make it through the summer.

Demi had been a member of the same singles group that XY and I had been part of. She left the group about the same time I did. We then began conversing on a more personal level, sharing thoughts and life events. We found we could confide bits and pieces with one another that only our therapists knew. It felt good to know someone else who was in counseling. Counseling is a great mystery to those who have never been. I know one woman who refused to go because "all the counselor will say is, 'cope with it' and I already know how to do that." Counseling, or therapy, is so much more than "coping with it." It is discovery and release; it is finding freedom and honesty. It is seeking life. With this common bond of counseling, Demi and I found a niche in which to let our friendship develop and blossom.

Yes, the gift of support came from many directions. I was truly blessed.

And don't forget Rose, the friend who spent the night with me before my first hospital stay. I won't forget. Thank you, Rose.

I believe I have found my me. I have a self that belongs only to me. My thinking is not overly tangential. I have discovered that I don't like meat in spaghetti sauce, but baby, keep adding those mushrooms! I no longer feel isolated from others or myself. I am whole in God's eyes and my own. I've discovered being human is okay. I do not have to worry about the horribleness of me. There is no terrible darkness to hide from. For when it comes right down to it, I don't think there is a deep, dark torturous terribleness about me. I am simply me. Best of all, I feel loved and capable of loving. That is good. Life is good.

When it comes to my shoes, I always know where they are. Every night, I put them under the footstool by my bed. Every morning, there they are! Ms. Woods would be so proud.

So Hannah Lee, I thank you:

Hannah Lee, P-H-D
I don't need
to hide and flee
Hannah Lee, P-H-D
See how I
take care of me!!

P.S. If I used to be discombobulated, am I now recombobulated?

Musings After the Fact: an epilogue

You will be secure,
because there is hope;
you will look about you and take
your rest in safety.

Job 11:18

Epilogue

Almost a year ago, I had my last therapy session. It turned out that Hannah Lee was right. When the time comes and you are ready, leaving your therapist and that all important therapeutic relationship is okay. (I cannot believe that I just admitted such a thing, and in public, too!) There are moments when I long for time with Hannah Lee, but mostly it is quite fine. I call her once in a while, and e-mail her regularly. She even e-mails me back. As much as I miss my dear Hannah Lee, it is neither frightening nor painful to be without her. I have handled the ever-present intense stress at work without feeling too overwhelmed or falling apart. It is rather nice.

The freedom I have felt these past months grows daily.

Thinking through all of this, I think that the most important change to come over me in my recovery is the lack of fear. I no longer live in constant fear of being found out. In fact, I rejoice in being able to share my story and not feel shame or fear. I am not afraid of myself, nor am I afraid of others.

Freedom from that constant fear allows joy to creep in with an ease I've never known before. I have boundaries enough to know what to share when and when not to share anything at all. I don't have the extraordinary unrelenting craving to be known and loved any longer. This, too, offers freedom.

Seldom do I fear other people or social situations. While I still have doubts and concerns about pursuing and developing new relationships, I look forward to the future opportunities that surely await me. Recently, I went to a party where I knew no one, not even the hostess. I had a great time. Gone was the always present repressing fear. Yes, I like this very much. Lack of fear is truly delicious.

Many discoveries have come to me during this past year. For instance, people have asked me how I did it, how I made it through. A clue came simply from looking around my house at books and musicals. Looking around, I realized that reading was one thing that kept me from going over the edge.

I never read anything too deep, but always had several novels and a biography or two going at the same time. Day by day, my love for reading and for old books kept me busy. I would read the same book over and over searching for clues to find me, longing for the life of various characters. My love for musicals also kept me going, especially the lighthearted ones such as "The Music Man," and "The Sound of Music." These interests proved to have been stronger than my mental illness. I often attempted to identify with the characters in both the musicals and the books, always looking for my missing identity and admiring their strengths.

Recently, I discovered another key to my recovery. So many people had listened to me. Doctors, psychiatrists, therapists—they all listened to me. But until a couple of people began *hearing* me, my symptoms had no place to go but downward. This doesn't mean people weren't doing what they had been trained for or that they were inept, but …. Then again, I think, was I hearing myself? Was I needing to listen to and hear myself before anyone else could hear me? Harry could not hear me until I was able to hear some of my noise in my head. Mandy thought she heard me when Vicki visited while I was under hypnosis. Her diagnosis brought me to Hannah Lee, the one who to my joy and chagrin, truly heard me. Perhaps hearing is the wrong term. Perhaps it is hearing with comprehension. Hearing with understanding. Hearing with empathy. All I know is that until people really could take in and work with what I was saying to them, very little progress was made.

Another discovery involves looking in the mirror. When I look in the mirror into my own eyes, I can see and connect to the nine-year-old me. I see that sparkle of joy, interest and delight in my eyes. I also see myself as a forty-six year old adult and embrace being that adult.

Delightfully and finally, I discovered why it was so important for me to have pictures in my mind—places for people to be and pictures of thoughts. It was the voices. With so many people talking inside of me, no room was left for other thoughts, so I made pictures. An amazing discovery. Amazing.

While I am now healthy in the mental health department, I continue to have small flare-ups of symptoms. Occasional thoughts still come that seem a part of my head, but not of my brain or mind. I continue to live through short periods of depression. Confusion comes too, at times. However, most of the time I am symptom free. Becoming used to the changes in my mind and body challenges me. For example, one of my medications was changed due to blood sugar concerns, and suddenly I am wide awake and filled with energy I haven't had for years. This energy pointed out some poor habits developed during my mental illness. I often had no ability to get myself into cleaning mode, or I would lay around for hours doing nothing. This is where musicals now come in handy. I can get a lot done to very loud musical CDs.

I also feel blessed that the right medications were found. I would really like to go off the medication some day, but am a bit fearful of returning to that mess that was once me. Recently, we did reduce the dose of the antidepressant. Sadly, I began feeling overwhelmed, and my thoughts grew a bit dark. Thankfully, Dr. Bestwell agreed to return to the higher dose, and my frame of mind returned to normal. Healthy normal, not crazy normal.

Yes, I do want to quit my medication, but, I do not want a repeat of hallucinations, dissociation, depression and not being able to differentiate between real and not-real. I want a life of realness to be experienced with a relatively clear head. This means I need to stick with the medications. Meds may or may not guarantee clearheadedness forever, but they sure are working now. As Hannah Lee has said, "If it is working, don't fix it." For now, I won't fix it. Medications are doing their job.

Last night I dreamed about XY. I think I can call him by name now without my heart cringing. Weston. Weston. In the dream, Weston marries a girl with his same wiry build and fair complexion. They look a bit alike. The mothers of Weston and the girl sit with me at a table a bit away from the couple, the newlyweds. Both mothers smile at me and say their thanks. The girl's mother gives me an afghan she has made in exchange for the gift I have given her daughter. Weston's mother simply thanks me for the gifts I have given her son, especially the gift of breaking open his shell of shyness. I woke up with more peace than I have had about Weston since that fateful night in November, 1990. Amazing how good it feels. Amazing how long it takes me to get over things. Best wishes, Weston.

In reality, I know little about Weston's life these days. I did meet up with him one evening and bawled my eyes out afterwards. I am okay—even with the tears. Pain just leaves me slowly. May happiness be his.

I feel very blessed these days when it comes to the men I know. Granted, they are all married, and some are family, but they demonstrate for me the realness of godly men. Through these men, I see the positives of relationship. I can admire how they relate to their spouses and other women. I am hoping these observances will guide me in my own future relationships. The way these men treat their wives is precious in my eyes. I am glad to have these men in my life.

Growing up I always believed I would get married, live on several acres of land and have an abundant number of children. So far none of that has happened. Until I realized that this single barren life of mine was truly a gift, I lamented over my existence. As I began to creep out of the fog of my mental illness, I began to thank God for my aloneness. I cannot imagine trying to manage a family while going through all the ick. I honor and commend those who have done it.

I don't know. Maybe my basically cheerful and positive core is what kept me alive and mostly safe. Perhaps there existed a battle between my more normal state of being and the chemical imbalance. I was born to laugh and smile and chatter. Did this innate part of me help me in the long run? Does this mean that personality is completely separate from mental illness? That is a thought worth contemplating someday. (Perhaps it could even become a doctoral thesis.)

In regard to the many hurts in my life: Once in awhile, I have wanted to seek blame for these hurts. But who would I blame? People have not hurt me with any harmful intent. People have just been people doing their best for their own survival. My own longing for approval and unconditional love combined with the chemical havoc of my brain led to my own internal responses to these hurts. I cannot take responsibility for the hurts brought on by others. If the chemicals in my brain were out of whack, do I still take responsibility for my internal responses to those hurts? A question awaiting an answer that may never be found.

At times, my emotions around being hurt stopped my own success at moving forward beyond the hurt. I would be furious with myself because I let the hurts have such power over me. So what was I to do with this? Dr. Phil would say, "Get over it." Once I could see myself and others more clearly, I was more able to "Get over it."

Yes, some of my odd quirks remain, and yes, sometimes I have difficulty differentiating between real and not-real, but these incidences are at such a low level they are usually not bothersome. If I have a memory and I cannot tell whether it is a dream or reality, I look at it from different angles to find discrepancies with reality. This seems to work. And again, I say: Life is good.

I feel good about my present life. I like myself. I like my quirks, my normalness, my me. In liking myself and my life, feelings that pop up now and again about various hurts are no longer needed. Hmmmm … Certain feelings about certain events are no longer needed. WOW! Oprah would call this an "Aha moment." Let me write that again: CERTAIN FEELINGS ABOUT CERTAIN EVENTS ARE NO LONGER NEEDED.

Hannah Lee, I think I have got it. Finally. Looking at the life I now lead, I have no need to carry and drag old feelings about old events around with me.

The past is neither my present nor my future. I can look past the hurts and say, "So there. I made it. I can smile real smiles. Hallelujah!" Life is good.

Which brings me to my heart's desire. Of course, I want to stay out of that dark hole of mental illness. Even more, I want my journey to mean something. I want my story to bring hope to others. I want people to know hope can become reality. I want people to know that being human and feeling the many nuances of each and every emotion can be good. I want people to know they are not alone. I want to give using the gifts God gave to me through this journey. "I want" with health. Life is good.

As I write this final paragraph, two years have passed since my last therapy session with Hannah Lee. I have recently begun seeing a new therapist. Today I realized there has been a part of me feeling shame in this, as if I have failed myself somehow. And yet, it is in reality another gift. A gift to myself. You see, some feelings of depression began creeping back a bit stronger and more often; also, I began to feel like the voices were thinking about coming back. Dr. Bestwell increased my anti-psychotic medication, which helped, but I thought more support might be good. Since I only want to move forward, and forward with hope, I sought the support of a therapist. It is strange but fun getting to know a new therapist. Some new ideas and thoughts have wiggled their way into my brain. This is good, very good. Yet, within this new relationship, a fear crept up—fear of being swallowed up by my therapist's opinions and thoughts rather than maintaining my own oneness and merely considering her opinions and thoughts. I think this fear is a healthy one rather than the overwhelming fears of my past. I am going to therapy to keep hold of my me—not lose it! Such a marvelous revelation to be gifted with. **I HAVE A ME FOR KEEPS!** Awesome. There is no shame here nor reason for guilt. I have not failed! This new round of therapy shall be to maintain and strengthen. I am glad of it. What a gift for life. What hope! Yes, life is good and I am fine. Hallelujah!

May the God of hope fill you with
all joy and peace as you trust in him,
So that you may overflow with hope by
the power of the Holy Spirit. (Romans 15:13)

ISBN 1412082013

9 781412 082013